The Christian Belief in God

by the same author

*

THE PROTESTANT MINISTRY
CONGREGATIONALISM

The Christian Belief In God

by
DANIEL JENKINS

FABER AND FABER
24 Russell Square
London

First published in mcmlxiv
by Faber and Faber Limited
24 Russell Square London W.C.1
Printed in Great Britain by
Latimer Trend & Co Ltd Plymouth

8｜7873
© *Daniel Jenkins*
1964

Contents

7

Contents

Preface

In the course of his memorable visit to the University of Chicago in the spring of 1962, Karl Barth described such questions as 'Does God exist?' as foolish. He went on to acknowledge, however, that we are all often guilty of the folly of asking such questions.

It must be admitted that this book is, from Barth's viewpoint, an exercise in folly. Yet I can plead in justification that, because we are all fools in this way, the writing of such books is a necessity. It may be true that to call God's existence into question is to indicate our infection with sinful rebellion against Him, to identify ourselves with the Psalmist's fool who says in his heart that there is no God. But is not this precisely the common situation of all men? The man of faith believes that God has taken pity upon the folly of His children and spoken to them in terms which their wayward minds are able to understand, through the foolishness of the Gospel. It remains hard, however, to avoid the possibility of folly when we take it upon ourselves to speak of God, even when we are trying, as we are in this book, to show how it is that the question concerning God's existence has been properly raised, and answered, not by foolish men, but by God Himself in His revelation.

God in Christ has borne with us in our folly. Perhaps I may gently observe that He has borne with us more patiently than has His servant, Karl Barth. For all the great bulk of his work, he has not always succeeded in making clear how God's Word in Jesus Christ speaks to men in their folly as well as in their need. Part of the consequence of this folly is that they do not always find it easy to reach the place where they can see how the judgment and forgiveness of God acts. They lose their way and spend their time becoming confused by questions which are of secondary and tertiary importance, and which are wrongly posed. It is surely part of our ministry to each other that we suffer each other's folly gladly and try to help each other through this confusion, so that we can define the right questions and hope to find the answers. The theologian should be particularly anxious to do this because, although he has less excuse for folly than any other man, he knows how easy it is to become en-meshed in the wrong questions. After all, many have believed that the ship of fools is manned chiefly by theologians.

The first point to be emphasized about this book, therefore, is that, since it deals with the fundamental human question, it is not written for theologians only. It is part of the distinctive folly of theologians to imagine that any book which deals directly with this question can be written only for theologians. The theologian, with all his technical equipment, exists, like the preacher, to help himself and other men listen to what God has said concerning Himself in His revelation. I am at one with Barth in maintaining that the only true way in which the question 'Does God exist?' can be answered is by giving heed to the initiative which He himself has taken in redefining and answering that question. Where I might differ is over the amount of discussion which is necessary to clear other matters out of the way before men, especially if they are not themselves theologians, can come to see the significance of the divine initiative.

The last thing which a book on this subject should want to claim is any great originality for itself. This is no more than yet another contribution to the on-going conversation about God and His ways. Its justification is twofold.

First, it is an attempt to bring together matters which are not always considered directly in relation to each other. If I am unhappy with Karl Barth's summary dismissal of unbelief, I am even more unhappy with the distinction which Paul Tillich draws between kerygmatic and apologetic theology. To make this distinction a sharp one is to misconceive the nature of the encounter between faith and unbelief. It overlooks the ambiguity of the position of the one who is involved in the encounter and fails to see all the complexities of the relation between faith and reason. It is also in danger of misunderstanding the nature of revelation itself. As we try to show in the fifth chapter, the testimony of Jesus himself to the divine reality is important evidence for the existence of God and not, as is often supposed, something which can be believed if we bring to it a belief in God which has been reached on other grounds. Unbelief is present in the hearts of believers, just as faith is also present in the attitude of many overt unbelievers, and the central affirmations of Christian theology cannot be made without facing the most radical objections to them. What is more, many of the greatest difficulties which faith has to overcome arise, not before people embark on the way of faith, but only after they have begun to make the venture. The chapters on 'Christian faith and human tragedy' and on 'The Justification of God' are largely taken up with these difficulties.

The other part of the justification of this book is that it is an attempt to consider the question of divine existence in a wider context than it is normally dealt with in academic circles. This is not to suggest for one moment that there is anything necessarily improper in the academic discussion of this question nor that this particular attempt can claim any immunity from academic criticism. It is a legitimate complaint against a good deal of modern theological writing that it imagines that it possesses this immunity, especially from the philosophical side. But it is true that the question concerning God's existence arises in different ways in different minds and the traditional formal discussion has tended to limit itself unduly to such matters as the status of natural theology and the relation between revelation and reason. This book tries to deal with these but it also tries to deal with difficulties which present themselves in less formal terms and also, as I say, with those which only arise when men have started on the life of faith.

The substance of some of the earlier chapters formed the basis of the Ayerst lectures at Colgate-Rochester Divinity School in the spring of 1960. It is a pleasure to recall my appreciation of the kindness and encouragement I received from the members of that great institution during my visit. I also expressed many of the ideas of this book, in summary and less developed form, in my short book, *Believing in God*, published by the Westminster Press, Philadelphia, in 1956.

I am particularly grateful to Dr. W. A. Whitehouse of the University of Durham who has made many useful suggestions and given me much encouragement, to Miss Joan Beach, who typed and helped revise the manuscript, and to Simon Jenkins, who prepared the index.

CHAPTER I

The Point of Departure

The Biblical view of the world in relation to God, is very different from that which it is often supposed to be by modern men. It is not that of a floodlit stage, where God is in the centre, visible to all who have eyes to see, and where all else stands clear and sharply-defined in relation to Him. It is that of a place of darkness and confusion of tongues, in which men are deeply conscious of their frailty and mortality and where it is hard to see what right and wrong are and what the meaning of life is. Light certainly breaks into this world and a voice speaks. It is a light which men discover to be sufficiently clear to lighten their path through life and it is a voice sufficiently precise to enable them to know with whom they are dealing and what His purpose for them is. But it is a light which shines in the darkness, a darkness which prevents many men from seeing it, and it is a voice which men, having ears, can fail to hear, even when it is the voice of the only-begotten of the Father.

To the men who wrote the most characteristic parts of the Bible, life was a mystery, whose meaning was not readily visible upon its surface. The answers to the fundamental human questions, 'Whence are we and whither do we go?' 'How shall a man know himself and how shall he live?' 'Is there a power not ourselves in control of all things to whom we are accountable?' are not self-evident. We can only hope to discover them if we move outside ourselves in response to a mysterious reality which cannot be fitted in to the rest of our experience, who

13

calls us forward into the unknown as Abraham was called or who compels us to turn aside, as Moses was compelled, to see a bush which burns and is not consumed. The Bible does speak of the establishment of a highway in which the wayfaring man, even the fool, the insensitive one who is unaware of the enigmatic character of existence, cannot go astray, but it is careful to insist that this way will not exist until the day of the Lord. Christians believe that the nature of that way is made clear in Christ but He Himself reminded us that the way which leads to life is narrow and the path strait. This refers not only to the possibilities of moral failure which are open to men but also to the intellectual obstacles which they encounter.

What is more, the light which shines in the Bible is one which is itself mysterious. Jesus speaks of the mystery of the kingdom and Paul frequently speaks of the mysteries of the Gospel and of central realities of faith, such as the relation which exists between Christ and the Church. What they mean is partly what we have already said, that the Gospel is not self-evident but presupposes the mysterious character of existence. It speaks out of the dimension of mystery. But they also mean that as men come to know it, as they are let into the secret, it remains mysterious because it comes from God, who remains in control. Through His revelation, men are taken into the counsel of God. As Jesus is made to say in the Fourth Gospel, they are no longer called servants but friends, whom the Lord consults concerning His will. But they remain *His* friends whom He consults after the manner of an Oriental monarch. He Himself does not become the 'friend' of man in this sense, man's counsellor and confidant about his own purposes.[1] The initiative remains with God.

The reasons for this lie deep in our understanding of the nature of the God revealed in Christ. He is, as the Bible constantly insists, the hidden God, whose thoughts are not as our thoughts nor His ways as our ways. We are estranged from Him, living in a world of darkness. We cannot, of ourselves, either think aright or handle the world around us aright. We are unable to look directly upon God's face and live, because we

[1] See *The Friendship of Christ* by Charles Smythe (Longmans, Green & Co.).

have lost the power to hold full and sincere personal communion with Him. When He calls us, we are aware of it as an
act of His electing grace. We are invited to have our place in His
purpose; we are unable to use Him as an instrument for the
fulfilment of our own. He invites us to consider with Him the
nature of that purpose and to know more and more about it,
but the condition of our being able to do so is that, at every step
of the way, we strive to realize the distinction between that
purpose and our own desires. He retains the initiative even in
revelation. The revelation of God vindicates itself as true revelation, in contrast to all natural forms of 'mystery-religion', such
as abounded in Jesus' day, by making clear that the God whom
it reveals is the hidden God.

When this is understood, the curiously broken, fitful, indirect
character of self revelation which God appears to adopt in the
Biblical story becomes more intelligible. This is very different
from the picture presented in some old-fashioned educational
courses in religious knowledge, where 'the idea' of God as a
general principle is alleged to be present in the consciousness of
mankind but is progressively developed and refined in the Bible,
with Isaiah emphasizing His holiness, Amos His righteousness,
Hosea His loving-kindness and finally Jesus His fatherly love.
Karl Barth, in his exposition of the doctrine of the Trinity at
the beginning of his *Church Dogmatics*, has shown how that
doctrine arose as an attempt to make clear how a God who
might be assumed to be unable to reveal Himself, in the sense
of imparting a share in His own life, to sinful man, nevertheless
does so reveal Himself and yet retains His essential lordship in
the revelation.[1] He retains this lordship not by holding anything
back from men which it is essential that man should receive but
by being fully Himself as Lord in His self-impartation. When
He takes 'the form of a servant' in Christ and exposes Himself
to the worst that men can do, it all happens according to His
'determinate counsel and foreknowledge' and when He gives
Himself to the Church in the form of the Spirit, the Spirit
retains the initiative. Men are placed at the disposal of the Spirit.

[1] *Church Dogmatics*, I, 1.

The Spirit is not handed over to their possession, as though they could act as God's agents, even in the impartation of the Spirit, apart from the Spirit's guidance. The Spirit leads and they follow. They do not automatically possess knowledge of the nature and will of God. They have actively to seek that will by asking, seeking and knocking, with all the recognition of their own imperfections and the vigilant self-criticism which these imply.

Revelation defines God as mysterious and it presupposes the mysterious character of existence. To recognize this is our proper point of departure. It is to possess that 'godly fear', that humble, cautious reverence in the presence of powers greater than we can comprehend, which the Bible in so many places describes as the beginning of wisdom.

It should be clear from the reference here to wisdom, as indeed it should be from our understanding of the concreteness and realism, one might almost dare to say the materialism, of the whole Biblical attitude towards life, that 'mystery' must be understood in a very different sense either from that of the irrational or the occult or that of a problem or a puzzle. God's revelation is not called mysterious because it cannot stand the scrutiny of daylight. It does not belong to the realm of the vague and the half-formed, to the twilight-world of experience lying below the threshold of consciousness which, when it is brought up into full consciousness can be adequately accounted for in other terms and controlled by being placed in a suitable, comfortable relationship with other aspects of experience. Men constantly try to do that with divine revelation and we shall be considering various modern attempts to do so later in our discussion, but in making such attempts we should be quite clear that we are refusing to accept revelation's account of itself. The mystery of revelation is, to echo some words of G. K. Chesterton, 'the mystery of daylight' itself. Whatever may be the relationship of Biblical revelation to other religious attempts to provide us with revelations of God, one thing stands out about the Biblical witness, and that is its openness, its precision, its personal and rational character. God's revelation comes not simply through events but through a particular interpretation of events. It comes through persons and a person who speak in language, so that in the Bible itself the nearest we can reach to a synonym for revelation is the 'Word'. It does not therefore need a carefully produced background in order to give it an illusion of reality while our critical faculties are dulled. We call it mysterious 'not because it offers so little to our understanding but because it overwhelms our understanding'.[1] The more precisely it is defined, the more rigorously it is examined, the more its essentially mysterious nature stands out.

When we speak of it as mysterious also, we wish to distinguish it from a problem or a puzzle. It is their inability to do this which makes it hard for many people who are trained in a scientific manner to grasp what Christians mean when they speak of the knowledge of God. The mysterious to most of us simply means the unknown. When we are able to understand how its parts are related to each other and how we can control them, its mystery vanishes. The problem is solved, the puzzle no longer worries us.[2] We can henceforward take the knowledge it provides for granted and need not go back to trouble ourselves over it unless it should happen to need revision in some respects in the light of further knowledge which has come to us. But the knowledge of God is both personal knowledge and decisive. It cannot be taken for granted. It cannot be mastered by us. We apprehend but never comprehend God. Yet it remains real knowledge because, as Augustine so movingly puts it, the more we know the more we realize there is to know. Asking, seeking and knocking, we are given answers, and yet they are answers which prompt us to further asking, seeking and knocking.

[1] G. S. Hendry, article on 'Mystery' in *Theological Word Book of the Bible* S.C.M. Press, London, 1950).

[2] The contrast between problem and mystery is discussed in an illuminating manner in the Gifford lectures of Gabriel Marcel, especially Vol. 1 of *The Mystery of Being*, Reflection and Mystery', Chapter 10 (Harvill Press, London), although his treatment suffers, after the manner of that of so many French Catholic philosophers, through an apparently incomplete awareness of the extent to which the Biblical understanding is one of mystery. It is a virtue of the treatment of mystery in Michael Foster's book, *Mystery and Philosophy* (S.C.M. Press, London), that he sees this so clearly.

The Point of Departure

It is essential to recognize that our knowledge of God and of the world in which we have our knowledge of God is of this mysterious character if the nature of the decision with which Christian faith confronts us is not to be misconceived. In fact, to refuse to see this is one of the most common, and most disastrous, sources of confusion and error in dealing with the matter of Christian belief.

Theology, and the community of the Church, are far from being exempt from this confusion and error. It is possible to think of and to present the Christian faith in ways which drain it of all mystery. Men can speak even of its central realities such as the cross and resurrection in a way which implies little awareness of the ambiguities and uncertainties which confront all who strive to discover ultimate meanings. The 'tragic sense of life' which is so pervasively present in the Bible is absent from their understanding, and with it all the light and the shadow of real experience. Their universe is all equally brightly-lit and every part of it is well-charted. Right and wrong are clearly discernible and the line between them in every situation can be nicely drawn. Heaven is as well-known as earth and commerce between the two is smooth and easy. God works according to rule and can be relied upon to respect the interpretation of the rules which His faithful servants have found to be most satisfactory in the course of long experience. The response of faith to such a God is not a leap into the dark, certainly no attempt to float on a sea seventy thousand fathoms deep. It is that of rational and sensible movement forward in the assurance that God will prove Himself to be as rational and sensible as His servant. Lack of faith does not mean the fear that in the darkness the light of revelation may cease to shine and leave us to despair. It means questioning the tried and tested interpretation of the route which is provided by God's authoritative spokesmen, who have definitive answers to all questions which can reasonably be asked, answers which are self-sufficient and need prompt no further questioning.

This is an attitude whose deficiencies can be fairly readily recognized and rejected when they appear in a particular individual. Few individuals have sufficient assurance and skill to cover up pomposity, banality and insensitivity under the cloaks of dignity and conventional wisdom for long. But these un-attractive qualities are not always so readily discernible and can be made to look much more inviting when they are displayed by spokesmen of institutions or theological systems, for the spokesmen are then able to point not to their own virtue or insight but to those of the institution or system. All who speak on behalf of churches which have even the formal adherence of large numbers of people and which have, therefore, developed a vested interest in maintaining an elaborate organization are peculiarly exposed to these dangers. It must always be one of the most damaging criticisms of the Roman Catholic Church that its spokesmen do so little to protect themselves against them and indeed seem frequently to regard it as a virtue of their Church that they are able to speak with such worldly self-confidence and freedom from self-questioning. They give the impression of knowing more about both heaven and earth than it is given to the rest of men, including those of the Bible, to know, and of being entitled to a certain complacency about such know-ledge. There are many Christians acknowledging allegiance to the see of Rome who are acutely aware of the mystery of revelation and walk humbly in its presence, but the customary style and tone of, for example, papal encyclicals suggest little awareness of what godly fear really means. And what holds for Rome holds much more obviously and crudely for Protestant fundamentalism and the more rigid forms of doctrinal ortho-doxy which are to be found in Protestantism.

Like most ecclesiastical temptations, however, this is not one of which the representatives of any theological tradition or school can claim to be free. Indeed, one reason why representa-tives of liberal schools or churches are often as vulnerable as anyone else to this temptation is that they believe that they have a vocational exemption from it. All institutions are inclined to become more interested in maintaining their own stability and coherence in this world rather than in following the light of the Spirit of Christ through all the dark places which otherwise we should prefer to ignore. They are all disposed to turn the great issues of faith into theological problems which, once the official answer in the textbook is provided, need not be reopened in any radical form. When this has happened, the mystery has been banished and things beyond all ordinary experience, which cannot be allowed for beforehand, like burning bushes, do not need to distract our attention from the routine business of living. For all the emphasis which the exponents of church institutions which speak with an authoritarian tone of voice lay upon the importance of the supernatural character of revelation, they have succeeded in naturalizing God. They have made over heaven into the image, if not of earth, then at least of their own institution. In doing this, they have taken away the sting, and the promise, of 'cosmic anxiety' more completely and successfully than any naturalistic philosopher.

Perhaps it needs saying that this is not meant to be an attack upon dogma as such. One of our main emphases will be upon the fact that revelation is of such a nature that it compels men to make a radical decision about God and the world and the person of Christ and the mission of the Church which they would prefer to be able to evade. What the classical dogmas of the Church are intended to do is to serve notice to all men who would follow Christ of the inescapability of these decisions. But Christians of all persuasions have not always seen with sufficient clarity that the necessity for these decisions cannot be laid down nor their precise nature defined in what we are accustomed to describe as a dogmatic way. Those who have known Christ are surely right to insist that the declaration 'Jesus Christ is Lord' faithfully describes that which is at the heart of authentic faith, and that certain inescapable conclusions follow if that declaration is accepted. Yet those who make this insistence should be the first to insist equally that it is impossible for anyone to believe that Jesus Christ is Lord unless he does so voluntarily from the heart and from the mind; and that means that they must have freedom to face and to overcome any objections raised by their hearts and minds to that belief. It is the way of humility as well as of pedagogic wisdom to accept many beliefs 'on authority' at certain times and on certain levels of experience. The words of the Bible, of the Church throughout the ages, of theological systems of tested value, deserve not only respect but also an attitude of expectant teachability in our approach to them which is not always forthcoming, and whose absence creates a great deal of unnecessary trouble. But the fundamental act of faith can never be simply a matter of the acceptance of the authority of a human institution. God in Christ requires a personal response, the honest, unreserved commitment of each individual at the centre of his being. Such commitment is impossible without critical awareness and a determination to be honest with one's own difficulties.

It has not always been observed that a certain kind of agnosticism is regarded by the men of the Bible as the most appropriate one in the presence of religious experience. This is not to say, of course, that it necessarily has much affinity with what is commonly called agnosticism today, which is often little more than a temporizing indecision in the presence of difficult issues, but it is sharply to be distinguished from the complacency and credulity which are assumed by some people today to be characteristically Christian attitudes. Man in the Bible is acutely aware of his limitations and his vulnerability. This is part of the concreteness and realism of which we have already spoken. 'God is in heaven, thou art on earth, therefore let thy words be few' says the preacher (Eccles. v. 2). Our attitude on this earth should be one of caution and vigilance, not seeking easy answers and realizing that one's enthusiasms and self-assertions, one's readiness to put one's trust in princes or in idols, is likely to prove misplaced. The fool who in his heart denies God is not the man who is so stupid that he shuts his eyes to a patent fact of common observation. He is the man who is so unaware of life's mystery that he can make dogmatic statements about its nature, on the basis of facts which are 'more plain than true'. He is the man who is so confident of his ability to find the answers quickly that he does not need to spend time in ensuring that he has properly formulated the questions. He is like the *phronimos* with whom Paul contrasts the true apostle in 1 Corinthians iv, the wiseacre who imagines that he does not need to be troubled by the perplexities and difficulties which beset those who try to follow the light of Christ through a world of darkness.

It cannot be too strongly emphasized that the situation which the Bible describes is not that of a divine revelation trying to convince the naturally critical intelligence of man of its authenticity. It is that of man confident of his own capacity and only too ready to believe that he is able to make his way through life on his own resources or with the aid of gods of his own invention, who is challenged and disturbed by a reality which breaks in upon him and upsets his complacency. When this man is able to accept this challenge and disturbance and acknowledge God, we are told by him that his faith is a miracle. This we often take to mean that it is not patent of rational explanation, but that is not what those who spoke of it as a miracle meant by it. They meant that it was not something they invented or found convenient but something which forced itself upon them, despite themselves, by the constraint of its reality. It spoke not to their 'will to believe'—it was that which led men to believe in idols— but to their scepticism concerning all the gods and all their own religious inclinations and institutions.

It can hardly be accidental that the first Christian heretics were called Gnostics, people who claimed to possess special inside knowledge of God and of His relation to the gods which gratified their sense of significance and made them feel sufficiently wise unto salvation without having to be plunged into the radical personal crisis concerning ultimate meanings out of which alone faith is born. They were able to speculate freely about the nature of God and of salvation because they were under no constraint to work out the implications of their belief in practice through an awareness of personal responsibility to the living God. This was in sharp contrast to Paul, who confessed to having been persuaded,[1] driven inescapably by the pressure of the facts, to the conclusion that nothing could separate him from the love of God. The attitude of Jesus in his humanity makes this decisively clear. As we shall see, this is part

[1] Romans viii. 38.

of the meaning of the dereliction and the cross—but it is also visible throughout His ministry, and not least in the parables. These were certainly not meant to be apt illustrative stories of general truths of common observation, although they are often understood in this way. Jesus spoke in parables not as a way of popularizing his basically simple message but in order to shake people out of the comfortable belief that they knew the will of God and were in process of obeying it. The parables describe situations which, on the surface, appear ordinary and familiar enough, but in which the will of God is shown to be the revolutionary and unexpected power which it is. It confronts reluctant men with the fact that God remains God in the mystery of His revelation, and that men are unable to comprehend and domesticate Him through their own categories. The point of the parables is not one which can be grasped by the type of mind which will 'believe anything'. They presuppose an analytical, self-critical attitude, the opposite of the worshipper of idols in the Old Testament and of the 'seeker after signs' in the New. The latter is precisely the man who has trivialized the relationship between God and man by trying to take it out of the dimension of the mystery of personal encounter in an enigmatic world into that of the subject-object relationship where he can be a judge and establish something of his own lordship.

Another way of denying mystery while remaining in the religious dimension is that taken by some theological liberals, who used to be more articulate in the last generation than they are today. These minimize the distinctive significance of the light which is in Christ by denying that the surrounding darkness is so very dark. There is no need specially to turn aside to see the burning, unconsumed bush because they see 'every common bush aflame with God'. There is no radical estrangement between man and God, which prevents us from reaching God through our own insight. There has been no Fall and there need be no salvation either. Jesus was certainly divine, but in the way in which we all are, only more so. There is no element of tragedy in life and, although we do indeed have many aesthetically stirring, morally elevating and even 'numinous' and 'mystical' experiences, their effect is to satisfy us with a sense of fulfilment rather than to disturb and challenge us. The divine on these terms is quickly absorbed into the human and, perhaps by way of a mystical pantheism, it quickly fades into the light of common day. This attitude has, in fact, a great deal of affinity with the humanism of those of artistic rather than scientific temper, and those humanists who have this view are probably right in saying that it does not seem to imply the need for a transcendent God.[1] The question we shall have to face is whether it does any more than give a gentle glow to the pale light of common day, leaving us with the need either to plunge into the realm of tragedy and mystery or to settle for the grey anonymity of ordinariness, in which we do our best to trivialize or ignore fundamental issues.

It is very interesting to observe here that both the great Greek thinkers who were aware of the mystery of existence and the early Christians were sometimes called atheists. The reason for this was that, in the ancient world, to believe in the gods generally meant to believe in powers and influences which belonged to this world, the world of subject-object relationships, and which were capable of being manipulated by men according to their own desires and needs. The great Greek thinkers knew enough to realize that the Supreme Being was not like that and Paul was not necessarily trying to use an apologetic device, an unsuccessful clerical gimmick, when he called the attention of the Athenians to the place of the unknown God. He rightly saw that their attempt to keep the throne of the universe vacant and their scepticism about the power of the gods might well prove to be their form of 'godly fear' and the beginning of wisdom. The Greeks who worshipped the 'unknown God' were not those to whom the preaching of the cross was foolishness. Much of our modern theological liberalism, and its related humanism, may have more affinity with the paganism of the ancient world than its exponents appreciate, and the fact that it appears in Christian or 'non-religious' guise may conceal from us the fact that all this has done no more than bring us back to the place

[1] See *Ecstasy* by Marghanita Laski (Cresset Press, London, 1961).

from where we started, and that we still need to inquire whether the transcendent God who has revealed Himself in Jesus Christ exists and speaks to us.

In view of the strictures which it is fashionable to pass upon the Puritan distrust of visual images and, indeed, of all conceptual images other than those chosen by God for the purposes of revelation, it is also worth saying that, in its origin, this distrust did not arise out of insensitivity to the mystery but out of a desire to preserve the true mystery of revelation from becoming domesticated and trivialized by human imaginations. Many of the Puritans may not have appreciated how complex the process of image-formation is and some of them were indefensibly heavy-handed in their treatment of 'graven images' in churches, but they were surely right in seeing that nothing is easier for men than to deny the real mystery of revelation by putting 'mysterious' objects and experiences which may be aesthetically pleasing or morally elevating in place of the encounter of man with God in His Word. The clean bareness of an old Puritan meeting-house, with the open Bible and the table of the Lord, reveals as much appreciation of the true mystery of the Gospel and, arising from that, the mystery of daylight, as the Gothic gloom and soaring vaults and sculptured niches of our cathedrals. Those who find these meeting-houses dull may do so because they have come together, not in order to discover and obey the will of the transcendent God who has revealed Himself in the man Jesus Christ, but in order to enjoy communion with the gods of this world.

II

It is, however, the more explicitly non-religious forms of denial of the mystery of human existence which assert themselves most emphatically in these days. Familiar as they are, their significance is not always very clearly grasped in relation to the Christian understanding of revelation. The most well-known, pervasive and aggressive of these attitudes is that positivistic one which takes into philosophy the approach to reality which its exponents believe to be appropriate to that of scientific inquiry. Its essence might be summed up briefly in the statement that life has no mystery, only problems, problems whose sole hope of solution lies in the application of scientific method in as many fields as possible. By scientific method, in its turn, they mean the method of experiment, observation, measurement and induction which receives its most complete exemplification in the physical sciences. Because the question 'why?' cannot be answered in these terms, it is dismissed as irrelevant. The only question which there is any point in asking is 'how?'

The strength of this attitude has lain in the fact that it has been able to point, with a great air of plausibility, to the dazzling achievements of the scientific method on those levels where it works well and to contrast these with the difficulties, ambiguities and conflicts which arise as soon as people move into realms where these methods do not so readily apply. The nearer one moves into the realm of ultimate meanings, with which, in their various ways, religion and the arts and the humanities all have to deal, the more striking this becomes. What more reasonable, then, than to conclude that this contentious and confusing realm is best ignored by sensible, practical men or, if that is impossible, that it should be firmly relegated to the margins of life, as a preoccupation of the leisure hours, in which the chief virtues to be displayed should be those of a playful and good-humoured tolerance?

It would be foolish, and irresponsible, for those who believe in the central importance of religion and the humanities to react against this attitude in a merely defensive way, as many of them have been accustomed to do for too long. After all, it has arisen in the aggressive form which it has, largely because those trained to try to take a synoptic view of reality have not made enough effort to relate truth derived from scientific discovery to truth derived from other sources. Also, there are undoubtedly large areas of life in which the question 'how'? is the only relevant one and where the way of responsible action is to follow scientific procedures as closely as possible. Yet, at the very least, it can be asserted that to assume that life has no mystery or that, if it has, its mystery is insignificant, is anything but the self-evident truth which the exponents of this point of view make it out to be. Indeed, to make such an assumption with the confidence with which it often is made, in the face of the overwhelming testimony of large numbers of people not notably deficient in intelligence, including scientific intelligence, to the contrary, is inevitably to raise doubts as to one's good faith in the matter. Who is being the obscurantist here? It is hard to resist the conclusion that what the scientific positivist is doing is no more than to make a gesture of impatience in the face of the highly-complicated relationship to the universe in which he finds himself. He tries to pretend that his world is simpler than it is, one in which he is not troubled by the burden of self-consciousness and by his mysterious relation to other selves which can never be adequately expressed or handled by scientific means. He does not want to be a man and tries to get out of his predicament by trying to persuade us all to settle for being computers.

This attitude represents a radical break not only with the religious but also with the philosophical tradition of the West, in fact with the whole circle of ideas which gave modern science its birth. 'The mystery of mysteries is that something exists.' It is out of an awareness of this fundamental mystery that we receive the impulse to seek knowledge. Where it is denied or treated as insignificant, our answers to the question 'why?', which we cannot help giving in one form or another, become increasingly ill-considered and imprecise and our search for scientific knowledge itself is in danger of losing its impetus.

On this level, the theologian and the philosopher should recognize that they are allies more frankly than they often do. A great deal of rude language has passed between them in recent times, and Reformed theologians have been among those most guilty of rudeness in this respect. It is true that the right relation between theology and philosophy is not easy to determine. The frontier between them is constantly shifting and it is inevitable that there should be frequent border disputes. Yet the theologian should understand, if he is a good theologian, that his ultimate enemy is not a philosopher but a false theologian, the devil who is expert at quoting scripture to suit himself and who is constantly at work in the theologian's own mind. To externalize the enemy as a philosopher is, perhaps, to fall into the devil's most subtle trap. It is also to conceal the kinship which exists between the philosopher and the theologian, which can help them, if both are judged and renewed by grace, to work as partners with different functions in a common enterprise. The polemic of modern Reformed theologians like Brunner and, to a lesser extent Barth, against the philosophers takes for granted their common awareness of the mystery of being. The modern world provides enough evidence to prove that this awareness is not one which can be safely taken for granted. This awareness on the part of the philosopher may also be nearer to the kind of awareness which constitutes the theologian's distinctive 'gift'— which is not, it need hardly be said, what justifies him in God's sight—than it has recently been fashionable for theologians to suppose.

Once again, it could be argued that the Platonic belief in the philosophical reason, which is sometimes regarded as an expression of the prideful spirit of man, might be equally well, and certainly more humbly and generously, interpreted as an affirmation of faith in the existence of meaning which could be an adumbration, in a world which knew not Moses and the prophets, of Israel's faith in the purpose of the living God. Werner Jaeger has suggested that Plato's enthronement of the philosopher-king in his ideal state when Athens was actually collapsing is a reminder of the faith of the prophets in Israel's God during her days of darkness.[1] Whether this is so or not, we are on firmer ground when we recall, as a Christian philosopher has helped us to, that the relation between the apprehension of life's mystery and the basic philosophical act is very close. 'To perceive all that is unusual and exceptional, all that is wonderful, in the midst of the ordinary things of everyday life, is the beginning of philosophy . . . Wonder acts upon a man like a

[1] *Paideia*, Vol. II, p. 262 (O.U.P., New York, 1943).

The Point of Departure

shock, he is "moved" and "shaken", and in the dislocation that succeeds, all that he had taken for granted as being natural or self-evident loses its compact solidity and obviousness; he is literally dislocated and no longer knows where he is . . . It is his whole spiritual nature, his capacity to know, that is threatened.'[1]

Pieper goes on to observe that it is extremely curious that this is almost the only aspect of wonder which comes into evidence in modern philosophy, and the old view that wonder was the beginning of philosophy takes on the new meaning that doubt is the beginning of philosophy. He protests that this does less than justice to what wonder does. For what it really does is more positive; it enables us to strike deeper roots. 'The innermost meaning of wonder is fulfilled in a deepened sense of mystery. It does not end in doubt, but in the awakening of the knowledge that being *qua* being, is mysterious and inconceivable, that it is a mystery in the full sense of the word; neither a dead end nor a contradiction, nor even something impenetrable and dark; mystery really means that a reality, the singular existing thing, is inconceivable, *because* it is the inexhaustible source of light and for ever unfathomable.'[2]

This may help to account for what lies behind the attitude of many modern linguistic philosophers, especially those who espouse logical positivism. Their work produces a curiously mixed impression upon the mind of the layman, such as the

[1] Joseph Pieper, 'The Philosophical Act', p. 135 of *Leisure the basis of Culture* (Eng. trans. Faber & Faber, London).

[2] See also P. Tillich, *Systematic Theology*, Vol. 1, (Chicago U. P. 1951), p. 110. 'The genuine mystery appears when reason is driven beyond itself to its "ground and abyss", to that which "precedes" reason, to the fact that "being is and non-being is not" (Parmenides) to the original fact (Ur-Tatsache) that there is *something* and not *nothing*.' He goes on, more controversially, to add that this is the 'negative side' of the mystery. The positive side becomes manifest in actual revelation. 'Here the mystery appears as ground and not only as abyss. It appears as our ultimate concern. And it expresses itself in symbols and myths which point to the depth of reason and its mystery.' Whether the relation between revelation and mystery can quite be dealt with in these directly 'negative' and 'positive' terms is doubtful, but it underlines the point that the *attitude* of the philosopher is very similar to that of the theologian.

present writer certainly is in this particular field. Much of it is the product of a fierce linguistic puritanism, which can only be carried on with this intensity by those who have a passionate faith in meaning, and therefore in mystery. This kind of puritanism should be particularly welcome to the theologian, who should be more conscious than any other man of how easily language can become distorted, corrupt and misleading, and who should always be prompted to revise, purify and deflate his own words in the light of the Word of God. Yet much of their work also gives the impression of being an essay in deliberate trivialization, the reverse of the process prompted by true philosophical wonder, that of trying to strike deeper roots. Could this be due to the fact that this philosophy is the reaction to an attack of radical philosophical unbelief on the part of those of philosophical temper, that it is a response to the threat of meaninglessness, the nihil? Because the nihil is intolerable, they fill up the void with exercises which provide strictly limited patterns of meaning and enable them to avert their gaze from the ultimate mystery. The curiously 'existentialist', almost 'eschatological', temperament of the great prophet of logical analysis, Wittgenstein, and his followers in the Cambridge of the 1920s, is hard to explain in other terms. If there is truth in this, there would seem to be little point in countering a flight from the threat of meaninglessness with rationalistic arguments which derive their force from the self-evident character of certain propositions made about reality, in the way in which Maritain does.

The threat of meaninglessness is undoubtedly real, and we shall have to try to consider it in a more direct form than this when we come to consider the cross of Jesus Christ. All we need to say now is that it is a threat which arises and can only be faced within the dimension of mystery. The trouble with most naturalistic philosophies, whether positivistic or not, is that since they are reluctant to recognize the status of the dimension of mystery, they make people reluctant to equip themselves with all the resources which are available in the experience of mankind to help them find their way about in that dimension.

The Point of Departure

This is perhaps the chief sense in which it can be said that the rise of modern science and of scientific ways of thinking has made it more difficult for the men of this age than for men of previous ages to find the way to belief in the Christian God. Belief has never been easy. It is an illusion to suppose that the men of the Bible and of earlier times, such as the thirteenth or the seventeenth or the latter part of the nineteenth century, possessed a gift of 'simple faith' denied to their peculiarly open-eyed and enlightened descendants in the twentieth. As we shall see, the most radical objections to Christian faith are expressed at the time of its establishment in the Bible itself. Yet it is true that the language and experience of the Bible need constant translation from those of their own age to that of others. After all, the institution of the sermon in the Church exists to remind us that this need is perennial. The problems of such translation will be more acute in one age than another. Ours is an age of such rapid change that it is not surprising that we should be particularly conscious of their difficulty. We might remember, however, that our resources for meeting these problems have increased along with the problems themselves. The forms of thought created by modern science do not make it easy for us to know what exactly happens in many parts of the Bible but our immensely improved methods of historical research, with the greater gifts of historical sympathy which they should bring, can help us enormously with our attempts at translation. What the aggressive confidence of scientific positivism has done, allied as it has been on more widespread levels by our concentration in the modern world on material advancement, has been to create certain psychological barriers to our giving the attention it deserves to the dimension of mystery. This means that many people have become inexperienced and incompetent in dealing with it, and therefore distrustful and on the defensive in its presence.

This is true not only in relation to religion and the Church, but also to all those fields where inter-personal relations are of primary importance, and these include politics and commercial life as well as the arts, the humanities and social life. All these require the acceptance of arduous and sustained discipline if understanding and competence are to be achieved in dealing with them, but people have often been too dubious of their status as genuine fields of human activity to devote the quality of attention to them which they readily expend upon science and technology. This lack of confidence has even infected the attitude towards their own subjects of those who have been specifically committed to theological or humane studies, with the result that they have tried to justify their existence by making their studies as much like scientific studies as possible, which in practice has often meant a retreat from mystery into triviality.

This means that we who belong to this generation should realize that, so far from being more discerning and enlightened than those of former times, we may be more inexperienced and more gullible. This should prompt us further to an attitude of great caution and humility in the presence of theological truth. To put the point in traditional Christian language, the chief way in which the devil tries to promote unbelief is not by putting questions into men's heads (especially those of 'modern' men) which God finds peculiarly hard to answer nor by giving them such strength of vision that they are able to look God straight in the face and put Him out of countenance; it is by distracting their attention from the whole subject. He tries to fill up the room of God, to crowd Him out of their lives, so that He appears unintelligible, irrelevant and unnecessary. This strategy has achieved some notable successes in the modern world, not least in the self-righteousness which it engenders in its victims. The trouble is, however, that the modern world is so dynamic and explosive that we cannot continue for very long without becoming conscious of our need for answers to ultimate questions. When we do, our danger then is that, in our desperation and inexperience, we try to take religious short-cuts, like the idolators of the ancient world. There is already plenty of evidence that this is just as much one of the dangers of the modern world as so-called 'irreligion'.

It is important, therefore, that we should recognize the reality and inescapability of the dimension of mystery as that in which the question concerning the reality of the Christian God arises and that we should have the humility, patience and receptivity which are necessary if we are to find our way about in it. We must not be intimidated either by the philistinism of a quasi-scientific positivism or by the two-dimensional rigidity of ecclesiastical orthodoxy from raising the most radical and far-reaching questions about life. It is right that we should ask why it is that we toil and suffer and sacrifice and rejoice. We need to know why we are made as we are, brought into being apparently fortuitously, as insignificant specks on a tiny planet in a gigantic universe of space and time, which we are yet able to comprehend with mysterious instruments we call our minds and to find adaptable to our little purposes. Why, creatures of a brief season as we undoubtedly are, do we long for eternity and believe that we were made for it? Why, although we are the seeming products of a process of natural selection broadly continuous with that of the non-human world, do we give such overwhelming and decisive priority to personal relations, whatever our professed beliefs, and act upon the conviction that it is in these that life's deepest and most enduring meanings are to be found? What is it which makes good to be good and evil to be evil and what is the source of our assurance that, in some sense, the distinction between them is bound up with the mystery of our existence itself? It is as foolish to maintain that we have no need to try to answer these questions as it is to pretend that the answer to them is self-evident and can be taken for granted. It is in relation to them that the Christian belief in God arises and the full meaning of that belief as an answer to them cannot be grasped if, for any reason, we are inhibited from asking the questions.

CHAPTER II

Belief and Honesty

To the extent to which their religion is genuine, men are never easy and at home in its presence. This has always been true, and it will remain true until the coming of the new Jerusalem when there will be no temple and, therefore, no religion. It is a mark of the unreality and lack of seriousness of a great deal of our modern thinking about religion that so many people should think of it primarily as a source of 'comfort'. It may often provide that, in legitimate and illegitimate ways, but to the extent to which men find it easy to be comfortable in its presence they have taken away its distinctive quality and tamed and domesticated it away from the realm of mystery. Karl Barth has defined religion in the sense of man's effort to reach out towards God as the enemy of true faith, which comes as a gift from God's side. What he means is that it is no more than an anxious attempt, whether in Christian or non-Christian guise, to 'square' God. Men go to considerable trouble and expense to keep God at a safe distance, so that He does not disrupt too radically their own conception of how they should live their lives. Whether this is an altogether adequate definition of the role of religion and of its relation to faith need not now concern us, but it certainly underlines the truth that God comes to men first as a challenge and disturbance rather than as a source of reassurance or as a fulfilment of their 'need for security'. Many forms of religion may be no more than projections of men's desires and hopes and such desires and hopes clearly become easily mixed up with their religion, but the nearer religion moves towards the God of the Bible the less possible does it become to sustain such a notion. Religion is a dangerous business to be mixed up with. When the God whom Christ reveals is encountered, the danger becomes mortal.

A good deal of time should, therefore, be spent in self-examination on the part of those who embark on a discussion of belief in this God. Here is a place, beyond all others, where the academic disinterestedness of the parties concerned cannot be politely taken for granted. It is a curious fact that while Christian preachers have long been accustomed to point out the obstacles created for belief by our reluctance to accept Christ's moral claims upon our obedience, Christian theologians have said very little about the operation of very similar considerations when the question of intellectual truth is being dealt with.

This remains the situation even today, when great attention is being paid to the sociology and the psychology of knowledge, often by Christian thinkers themselves. There has, it is true, been a fair amount of study of the sociology and psychology of religion, but the weapons used in these studies have rarely been turned upon the theologians, or the anti-theologians, themselves. Yet we have become familiar with the ways in which our thinking is deeply influenced, if not completely motivated, by deep urges of pride or timidity or self-assertion or by desires for security, acceptance or prestige. Human thinking is shot through with rationalizations which can achieve extraordinary degrees of subtlety and elaboration. This can happen not only with individuals but also, and often more effectively, with communities. Rationalizations can become ideologies, which have power to grip people over many long generations and which can invoke many kinds of sanctions to prevent their own overthrow. Where religion and man's 'ultimate concern' become involved, the tendency to rationalize and form ideologies clearly becomes greatly intensified.

The fact that the human mind works in this way has not, of course, escaped the notice of critics of religious belief in general and the Christian faith in particular. One need only recall the Marxist dictum that 'religion is the opiate of the masses'. That particular argument represented a peculiarly dubious piece of social observation since, on the whole, the classes have inclined to use religion as an opiate much more than the masses, especially in modern industrialized and urbanized societies, and religion appears to have a powerful deproletarianizing influence. Yet that there is a large element of rationalization and ideology-formation in religious thinking has been sufficiently obvious to occasion a great deal of comment. What is surprising, rather, is that it has not aroused more. The critics of religion in our own time seem to have been curiously reluctant to use this weapon. If Feuerbach were alive today, he would surely have been able to produce a far more deadly analysis of what passes for Christian faith in God than he was able to a century ago, aided as he would be by all the apparatus of modern psychology and sociology. All those presentations of the Christian faith which drain life of its mystery, of which we spoke in the last chapter, are peculiarly vulnerable from this point of view, especially when they have become articulated in long-established institutions. Yet it has been left to Karl Barth, the church theologian, to call attention to the merits of Feuerbach's polemic and to use it as an instrument of ecclesiastical self-criticism.[1]

Perhaps, however, it is not so surprising, on reflection, that the opponents of Christian belief have shown this curious reluctance to use these weapons. They cannot be without a suspicion that they are double-edged and that they themselves can be cut as they try to wield them. Theologians may often be guilty of rationalization and the defence of ideologies, but is it self-evident that their critics are immune from such temptations? Yet it is remarkable how often the critic of Christianity finds it hard to resist drawing invidious comparisons between himself as a clear-eyed and open-minded independent thinker, able to look reality in the face with a cold, unbiased eye, and the miserable, gullible, irretrievably prejudiced publican of a Christian.[2]

---

[1] See *The Essence of Christianity* by Ludwig Feuerbach, with an introduction by Karl Barth (Harper's Torchbooks, New York).

[2] Thus, we may entirely agree with Sigmund Freud when he says, 'Where questions of religion are concerned people are guilty of every possible kind of

Belief and Honesty

This has been an attitude peculiarly characteristic of unbelieving scholars in universities in recent generations, partly because of the combination of social circumstances which produced a sub- or an anti-intellectual Pietism on the one hand and the philosophy of the Enlightenment on the other, which often met in the same families and the same institutions. These scholars have sometimes proceeded on the assumption that whereas theological faculties were dominated by vested interests and operated in blinkers, their own departments of scholarship were islands of sweetness, light and open vision. It is surely obvious that rationalization, ideology-formation and the establishment of vested interests, go on in every sphere of life and every department of scholarship. Nothing is harder to achieve than genuine disinterestedness. What can be said with certainty is that the man who assumes that his own disinterestedness can be taken for granted, whether as a theologian or as an anti-theologian, has failed to meet the first condition of being able to achieve it.

The old theologians undoubtedly claimed too much and over-simplified the situation when they claimed, as they often did, that atheism was due to moral corruption.[1] One of our main contentions in this book is that there are great difficulties in the way of faith, difficulties which loom the larger the further one proceeds along the road of faith. These difficulties orthodox theologians have not always properly faced, because of inadequate identification with the suffering of their Lord. But the old theologians were not being merely truculent and self-righteous when they said what they did. They were partly looking at the atheists whom they knew in their own hearts. Whether Pascal was speaking the whole truth or not when he said that the difficulty we have in believing is only the difficulty we have in obeying, it is remarkable how easy it is in this realm

insincerity and intellectual misdemeanour', but we note that the only illustrations he gives of these are from people who are well-disposed to religion. (See *The Future of an Illusion*, pp. 56-7 of English translation, Hogarth Press and Institute of Psycho-Analysis, 1928.) Is no other form of 'insincerity' possible or worth mentioning here?

[1] Calvin, *Institutes*, Book I, Chapter 4.

37

in particular to become more interested in one's own personal standing in the debate or in the impression one is making upon one's fellows as a man of sensitive imagination and enlightened sentiment than in trying to seek and follow the truth.

This is why the believer is at least entitled to ask the opponents of the Christian faith to offer more evidence of their intellectual good faith than they are. often ready to provide. The one great advantage which the believer has over his uncommitted adversary is that his faith is always driving him to seek understanding and showing him that understanding is impossible without self-examination and self-criticism. God desires truth in the inward parts and, whatever the unbeliever may think, the believer knows that God is not deceived by professions of belief which are not sincerely made. These professions cannot be sincerely made unless the objections to them are honestly faced. But the unbeliever is unable to invoke this kind of support and is constantly being thrust back upon himself. That this is not the whole truth about his situation, and that he is in contact with God whether he is prepared to admit it or not, is what makes conversation with him possible and hopeful from the believer's point of view. But it certainly does not encourage the believer to accept at its face value the contention he is constantly disposed to make that, as an unbeliever, he is automatically likely to be more disinterested than the believer. To accept that is to accept unbelief, for it implies that God is not the truth and that we have independent standing-ground where truth stands out more clearly than in conversation with God. This is to deny Christian experience.

Nor should delicacy of feeling allow us to leave the directly and vulgarly moral factor entirely out of account. The fact that this argument is used with too great facility, and sometimes unscrupulously, by evangelists whose zeal outruns their humility does not invalidate the measure of obvious truth which it contains. It is the fact that we are all so vulnerable at this point which makes it hard for such evangelists to resist the temptation to use it improperly. We look around for reasons to deny God's existence because that is a way of avoiding having to leave our selfish and evil courses and to live in love and charity with our neighbour. To seek for confirmation of the truth of this, the believer will know that he need look no further than his own self as he struggles between faith and unbelief.

Attention is not called to these points simply in order to provide an *argumentum ad hominem* for Christian apologists. To derive much satisfaction from such proceedings would indicate that the apologist had fallen into the same trap as his opponent. In such conversations, it is essential that we should always remember that each one of us is an unbeliever at certain times or in some aspects of his experience and that those who make open professions of unbelief are men of like nature with ourselves who are making explicit their awareness of obstacles to belief which are present in the minds of believers also. What we wish to emphasize is how difficult it is for all men, professed believers and unbelievers alike, to achieve disinterestedness or impartiality in dealing with the truth or otherwise of the Christian faith and how necessary it is for us to bring out into the open the question of what our motives are, so that they can, at least, be submitted to the most searching examination of which we are capable. The history of theology and of church institutions, not to say the testimony of the Bible itself, proves how easy it is to turn even faith in the living God into a form of human ideology.

Unless the need for self-criticism is clearly seen, the possibility of reaching real faith in God who is the Lord is doomed to failure. This is true, once more, just as much if faith is approached from the point of view of a complacent or defensive orthodoxy as it is if it is approached with the closed mind of militant unbelief. Modern philosophy has been described by H. A. Hodges as suffering from a crisis of presuppositions. We can no longer take for granted a common way of looking at the world, with the result that communication between people of different schools is extremely difficult and rarely creative. We disagree, in T. E. Hulme's familiar phrase, not only about doctrines, about what we say we see, but about dogmas, what we see through in order to see at all. This crisis is at its most acute when the question of belief in God is raised, yet it is of its nature that it is here, more than anywhere else, that people are unable to stand outside themselves and examine their dogmas.

The need for sharp self-awareness and self-criticism is still further underlined when the second consideration which should be before us in considering belief in God is borne in mind. It is that it requires careful checking to ensure that one is genuinely facing the question concerning belief in God and not a quite different one with which it has become closely associated. Christian revelation comes in a particular historical dress, that of the Bible and the Church throughout the ages, and it comes to each individual even more particularly, through churches and other individuals claiming a Christian name who have influenced him. This is inevitable if what we are dealing with is a movement in the personal dimension which genuinely breaks into human history rather than a set of general principles, but it means that a disciplined effort of critical attention is required if the essence of the faith is to be distinguished from ideas, attitudes, practices, loyalties and interests which have gathered round it and bear some relation to it.[1] The late C. E. M. Joad, before his conversion, was in the habit of making the complaint that when people made damaging attacks upon Christianity, Christians tried to get out of it by saying, 'But that isn't *real* Christianity'. Irritating though it may be, that is often a perfectly true answer, especially in these days when people and things are known by their public 'images'. Bertrand Russell, one of the most persistent critics of Christianity, frequently gives the impression, for example, that he is constantly reacting against the rather stuffy Evangelicalism of his grandparents' day rather than trying to make up his mind about the faith of the New Testament. And in a revealing review of a reissue of Samuel Butler's 'The Way of All Flesh' written in the London *Observer* shortly before his death, Bernard Shaw confessed that many of the young intellectuals of Victorian England seized eagerly upon Darwin's theory of evolution, not because they

[1] So far from making it a rule to believe a thing because you have heard people say it, you must not believe anything without behaving as though you had never heard it. (Pascal, *Pensées*, p. 209, No. 374 (Harvill Press, 1962).

were convinced by it, but because it was a convenient stick with which to beat the clergy of their day, whom as a social group they heartily disliked and whom they took to stand for Christianity. It is not easy to understand what the Christian faith really is. The only way to do so is to stand alongside Jesus Christ as the Bible witnesses to Him, in the way in which we shall go on to try to do, and to reject all images of the Christian faith which we have which are not conformed to that. When we do so, much of what passes both for Christian belief and for rejection of that belief will have to be looked at in a new light.

Once again, even when the ill-disposition of opponents of the Christian faith is allowed for, the Christian churches themselves must be prepared to accept a large part of the blame for the peculiarly widespread confusion about the nature of the Christian faith which exists in these days. The churches themselves have not sufficiently appreciated how difficult it is for sinful men to understand the Christian faith and to achieve the simplicity of spirit and singleness of eye of the Gospels. With the best will in the world, they have naturally been anxious to commend their faith to the largest number of people possible and, in the process, they have often been tempted to sacrifice the profundity of truth to superficial attractiveness. And they have often used the very instruments which lie to their hands to safeguard themselves against these temptations as means through which they fall headlong into them. They have failed to see, for example, that part of the purpose of the sermon in church is not to try to gain and hold the attention of people at any price but to help the Church so to listen to the Bible that it is led away from misunderstanding to hear afresh the authentic Word of God. This is why it is essential that, lying behind the Church's preaching, there should be the critical discipline of dogmatic theology, in which the church checks her proclamation to help ensure that when she preaches, it is the real Word of God and not the words of men pretending to be that Word which is being heard. When the Church's preaching is understood in this way, it should become a real source of self-criticism and renewal. It is designed to prevent the preconceptions and sectional interests and prejudices of that particular group of people in that particular place from getting in the way of the true showing forth of the authentic Christ. This is why the sermon is meant to be the most critical, the most disinterested and most responsible form of Christian utterance.[1] The fact that it is often thought by men to be the least is an indication of how far the churches misunderstand their proper function in these days.

What we are saying, in effect, is not much more than that it is important for the reflective person to have some knowledge of theology before trying to make up his mind about the Christian faith, enough, at least, to distinguish between the central realities of the Christian faith, 'the apostolic tradition' itself, and the various ecclesiastical and theological traditions which have arisen out of it and which have been so vigorous in the history of the Church. That may seem an extremely trite observation to make, but the state of discussion of these matters in the modern world provides us with ample illustration of the fact that it is worth making. Quite apart from all the difficulties about reaching disinterestedness which we have already mentioned, it is also temptingly easy to make up one's mind about Catholicism or Fundamentalism or Classical or Liberal Protestantism and to imagine that this is the same as making up one's mind about the claim that the living God has spoken His decisive Word in the man Jesus Christ.

An example of the subtle ways in which this way of thinking can lead us astray is provided by this quotation, which is worth making because it occurs in a book which is otherwise ex-

---

[1] It is this which lies behind the claim of Barth and other Protestant theologians that a 'kerygmatic' presentation of the Christian faith is the appropriate one in every situation and that 'apologetics' should not be thought of as a preliminary discipline which is necessary to clear the ground before the Gospel can be heard. The Gospel itself clears the ground and men cannot present it to themselves and to their neighbours without trying to deal with that which contradicts it in their own experience. Having said that, however, we must go on to say that the trouble today is that the nature of kerygmatic preaching is widely misunderstood and that when people hear what many preachers actually do in their sermons they are quite right in reaching the conclusion that something more and something different needs to be done.

tremely perceptive, 'But for many of us today, I fancy, a real orthodox theist is a little like a Jacobite. We do not, unless we are clergymen, speak of God unquestioningly, as a matter of course; and the clerical fashion of doing so seems to us slightly quaint. And even with Kierkegaard, we saw, God is no longer in the centre. It is not so much His presence we are made to feel, as despair at the failure to reach Him over an infinite gulf; it is less faith than the will to faith.'[1] It is no wonder that Mr. Ussher should do less than justice to Kierkegaard's understanding of faith because he has set up the man of straw of the conventional 'real and orthodox theist'. Surely, the whole question is begged by calling such a man a *real* theist'. The clerical fashion of speaking of God unquestionably and as a matter of course may reasonably seem to him to be slightly quaint but by assuming that this is a mark of 'real theism', Mr. Ussher avoids having to face the possibility that such a way of speaking, in our situation, would have seemed even more quaint to the men of the New Testament. Thus the question concerning the nature and challenge of faith is neatly evaded, even in a discussion of Kierkegaard.

There can be little doubt that one of the greatest sources of confusion in present-day discussion about belief is that the religious faith about which many people make up their minds, whether positively or negatively, is not the same as what the men of the Bible say is produced by the revelation of God in Christ. This is true even when all due allowance is made for the different dress which the same reality may wear in differing situations. This need not happen. All reading of the Bible is selective and there will always be discussion as to whether this or that interpretation of it is the right one. But sufficient unity exists among those who devote their attention to these things to enable us to say that the main lines of what authentic Christian faith is can be clearly drawn from the Bible, and that they are different from what men often suppose them to be. It is, at least, reasonable to ask all who want seriously to make up their minds

[1] Arland Ussher, *Journey Through Dread*, p. 123 (New York, Devin Adair, 1955).

about these matters to give careful and critical heed to what Jesus Christ, as the Bible presents Him, says.

A third consideration deserves mention, which may be of less importance in the academic discussion of these matters but which is a fruitful source of confusion on the practical level. It is that people are often disposed to think of 'religion' and Christian faith as substantially the same, or at least of the one simply as a subsection of the other, so that if one is in favour of religion in general it can be assumed that one is likely also to be in favour of the Christian faith also. It is true that when people speak of 'religion' in this way, they mean to use it as a synonym for Christianity, together perhaps with the modern Judaism which is closely related to it, but this still creates a dangerous ambiguity. Man may be incurably religious. To the extent to which he is indifferent to religion, it could be argued that he is something less than human. But this does not mean that all religion is the same as faith in the Christian God. Once again, 'Religion is the enemy of faith.' There is nothing about which the Bible is clearer than that it is not our religiousness, nor our related awareness of the dimension of mystery in itself, which justifies us in God's sight. Man's religion, even when it bears a Christian name, stands in need of redemption by the grace of God, like every other part of his life.

The peculiar danger which arises in Western society when men fail to see this—the danger may be different in communities where the dominant forms of religion are non-Christian—is that people give approval to the religious enterprise without regarding what it deals with as being concerned with the ultimate and decisive. Religion in this situation becomes religion without God, at least God in the Biblical sense of the One who determines all existence and to whom all men are answerable. The God of such religion is the private point of reference of those who are 'interested in religion' or a general symbol of the various forms of human aspiration. He is an 'optional God'. Religion conceived in such terms is clearly a barrier to knowledge of the one true God. It can, of course, be argued that this conception of religion is correct and that its popularity among so many people in these days is a consequence of the inevitable relativizing of our concept of God which has taken place in the modern world. But, as we shall be trying to show in our last chapter, it has to justify itself against an interpretation of the meaning of faith which is radically different and which has this claim upon our attention which cannot be evaded, that it is also the claim of the Founder of the Christian religion and of his original followers. It is inexcusable for anyone to assume that he is making up his mind about the truth or otherwise of the Christian faith when he is making up his mind about religion as a human activity in this way. Christ claims to be the truth, decisive reality, and the God of whom He speaks purports to be the God of all men. Those who are prepared to accept Christ but not to accept his central message have, at least, the obligation to recognize that they are asserting that He is radically mistaken. Honesty demands that we acknowledge that Jesus knew what He meant and that we take seriously the convictions for which He went to the Cross without trying to substitute others which we find more acceptable and then to wish them on to Him. The question of belief in the Christian God cannot be decided unless a determined effort is made, with a full awareness of the complexity of the task, to discover what Jesus Christ would have us believe about that God.

CHAPTER III

Revelation and Reason

———————

The history of Western thought is full of attempts to show that the existence of God can be proved by the unaided reason of man, reflecting upon the nature of internal human experience and observation of the external world, without taking into account the specific data provided by Christian revelation. Most of these efforts, like so much in Western philosophy, can ultimately be traced back to the Greeks, and in particular to Plato and Aristotle. They reached their distinctive form, however, within the Church itself, and, in particular, the Church of the Middle Ages. It was at this time that the best-known proofs for the existence of God received their classic formulation, and they still have great influence upon the thought of the Roman Church. Their exact status is a matter of active debate among Roman Catholic theologians. In official teaching, they are, of course, never regarded as being more than at best supplementary to truth given in revelation. Some theologians, in effect if not always in so many words, give them a status very little different from that which will be suggested for them in this chapter. The fact remains, however, that the Roman Church does make it an article of faith that God's existence can be demonstrated by the unaided reason of man and, in practice, a considerable vested interest has been built up in maintaining the version of these proofs which is to be found in Thomas Aquinas. St. Thomas's five proofs are still given as part of the normal first instruction to converts and a large part of popular expositions of Thomism is often taken up with their defence. This is not always done with close attention to these arguments in their natural setting and the question is only sometimes raised whether they might not have very different connotations within a Christian context from those which they had among the non-Christian Greeks.

Whether the Reformers of the sixteenth century regarded it as possible to prove the existence of God by the unaided reason of man is a matter of fierce debate. The relevant passages in Calvin are open to a variety of interpretations, but many of the Protestant Scholastics clearly considered 'rational theology' to be a possible enterprise. Barth is right, however, in emphasizing that, compared with theologians who came before and after, the theologians of the Reformation showed little interest in the possibilities of natural or rational theology. It was not until the rise of the Deists and, to a lesser extent, the Unitarians, that much stress was laid on rational theology, and this was often in conscious opposition to the dominant tradition of classical Protestantism. The whole discussion was put upon a new basis by the much greater emphasis on subjectivity characteristic of the Romantic Movement, as exemplified in different ways by Kant and Schleiermacher. Since Schleiermacher, and until the rise of Barth and the rediscovery of Kierkegaard and changes of philosophical climate in the directions of existentialism and linguistic analysis, the dominant emphasis in Protestant theology has been upon demonstrating the validity of religious experience rather than upon proving the divine existence independently of that experience.[1]

It is not within the purpose of this book nor the competence of its author to explore in any detail the ground covered by what is called 'the philosophy of religion' in the West. The practitioners of that philosophy have the right to complain, however, that those whose interest, like that of the present writer, lies chiefly in the exposition of revelation in its own terms, often do not define their position with sufficient sym-

[1] See *Studies in the History of Natural Theology* by C. C. J. Webb; *The Interpretation of Religion* by J. Baillie; and *Types of Modern Theology* by H. R. Mackintosh.

pathy and care in relation to the issues with which they concern themselves. There is a breach of fellowship here which cannot altogether be excused by the fact that disagreements are often sharp. A measure of goodwill and fellow-feeling should surely arise among all who are prepared seriously to raise the question concerning divine existence. Theologians have no more right to rule out as inadmissible in advance certain contributions from the philosophical side than philosophers have a right wilfully to misunderstand what theologians are saying because it is not expressed in categories with which they are most readily at home. The theologian has an obligation, therefore, to state his attitude to the traditional philosophical proofs of God's existence in as constructive a manner as possible. If he does not find them acceptable, he must still try to evaluate their significance. To do less is to be guilty of the arrogance of which he often accuses the philosopher, and arrogance is the least pardonable of sins in the theologian.

I

Three points relevant to our discussion can be made about the complex of issues which are normally gathered together under the heading of natural theology. The first is the least controversial. It is that their significance for the Christian understanding of God is likely to vary greatly according to the situation in which the issue arises. As we have already hinted, arguments for divine existence, such as the cosmological and teleological arguments in Aristotle, may have a quite different significance in an ancient Greek context from what they have as part of a Christian theological system. Is it enough to say of those who did not know Christ but who yet said that the world must have had a Creator and that its organization pointed to an end other than itself that, in saying so, they were giving expression only to the spirit of human self-sufficiency? Similarly, there are many men in the modern world as well as in the ancient who have never effectively heard of Christ or who, for various good or bad reasons, have not been able to give serious heed to the Word of God as declared by the Church. Yet they have some sense of the mysterious character of existence and are unable to deny the possibility that the world within and around them points to a reality beyond itself. Is it improper to start from this awareness in talking with them and to ask them whether it does not, in some way, raise the question of God?

This question must be sharply distinguished from that of the status of any so-called 'natural' knowledge of God in a systematic exposition of the Christian faith. Here the warnings and even the vehement denials of Karl Barth and others may have a great deal more to be said for them. To be able to maintain a natural theology alongside a theology of revelation with little sense of their incongruity, if not radical incompatibility, does suggest that we do not trust the testimony of God in His revelation and that we are trying to domesticate God in a subordinate place in a universe in which man is at the centre, even though that may be the reverse of our professed intention. The reality of the Christian experience of God is called into question if a theological system starts under the apparent necessity to prove that the God who has chosen to reveal Himself to man in His own time and His own way nevertheless needs to have His existence demonstrated by human ingenuity on the basis of a view of the universe which ignores the data of revelation, before even those who claim to believe in that revelation can bring themselves fully to believe that it has taken place. Kierkegaard's famous protest against such a procedure is unanswerable.[1] At the same time, we are capable of looking at the world of subject-object relations in such a way that we are not immediately aware of personal encounter with God on the 'existential' level and when we do so, there are considerations which present themselves to men, believers and unbelievers

---

[1] 'So rather let us mock God out and out as has been done before in the world—this is always preferable to the disparaging air with which one would prove God's existence. For to prove the existence of one who is present is the most shameless affront, since it is an attempt to make him ridiculous.' (*Concluding Unscientific Postscript*, p. 485.)

alike, which raise questions in their minds which require an answer. It is very possible that an adequate answer cannot be given without invoking what we learn from revelation but this does not mean that it is not worth looking at how the questions arise and asking whether they are proper questions.

This is particularly true in the case of the two best known of the traditional 'proofs' or 'demonstrations' of the existence of God, the cosmological and the teleological. The cosmological argument starts from common-sense observation of the world around us. Everything appears to have its cause in something else, by which its existence is determined. This cause is itself the effect of another cause, and so on apparently *ad infinitum*. Because everything is conditioned by that which precedes it, it must be seen to be contingent. Everything we know in ordinary experience is relative to something else, upon which it depends for its existence. Nature is to be understood as a system of relations. So far, there would be widespread agreement, whatever qualifications the cautious might wish to make in the notion of causality for the sake of complete precision of scientific statement. The further conclusion drawn from these widely-agreed conclusions by the exponents of the cosmological proof is, however, much more debatable. Does not this endless chain of causes necessarily imply a primary cause which potentially contains all these effects—the unmoved Mover, whom men call God? It should be noted that the argument does not necessarily claim that we are able, by empirical experience, to reach the unmoved Mover simply by following the chain of causality to the end. That is impossible because of the very nature of the chain. There is no end. What it does say is that the system of causal relations carries within it the clear implication that there must be an unmoved Mover. Otherwise, we should be left with *mere* contingency. There is no meaning in mere contingency and yet we find meaning. As Fr. Coplestone puts it in his discussion of Thomas Aquinas's version of the cosmological proof, 'It is the problem arising from the existence of finite and contingent Things at all which most clearly points to the existence of a trans-finite being. . . . One can hardly admit that the existence of finite being at all constitutes a serious problem and at the same time maintain that the solution can be found anywhere else than in affirming the existence of the trans-finite. If one does not wish to embark on the path which leads to the affirmation of transcendent being, however the latter may be described (if it is described at all), one has to deny the reality of the problem, assert that things "just are" and that the existential problem in question is a pseudo-problem. And if one refuses ever to sit down at the chess-board and make a move, one cannot, of course, be checkmated.'[1] What we take to be asserted here is that, at the very least, although the cosmological proof may not be in the strict sense a proof, it is a powerful reminder that we are creatures who are impelled to find meaning in the contingency of the system of relations in which we live and that that meaning must transcend the system.

This assertion becomes more explicit when we consider the argument which has always had the greater popular appeal, the so-called teleological argument. That the universe displays to our eyes the most amazing order and design is undeniable. The scientific positivist who firmly resists all invitations to make the leap from the internal system of relations which he finds within the world to that first cause of which the cosmological argument speaks has, all the same, to admit that there is the most remarkable correspondence between human minds and the structure of the universe as it presents itself to human experience, a correspondence which alone makes the researches of the scientist himself to be possible. As Erich Frank puts it, 'Has modern science not proved that nature follows exact mathematical laws —that its seemingly chaotic processes actually are subject to a most amazing mathematical order and harmony?'[2] However incomprehensible the primary cause of the universe may be, surely it must have some rational character, conformable and akin to human reason?

There is not only order. What has impressed many people even more strongly with the sense of transcendent meaning is

[1] *Aquinas*, pp. 123–4 (Penguin Books, 1955).
[2] *Philosophical Understanding and Religious Truth* (O.U.P., 1945), p. 30.

the fact that there is also beauty. Is it conceivable, we all ask when we have been deeply moved in its presence, that a lovely countryside, bursting with fresh life in spring-time, is the product of an entirely fortuitous collocation of blind forces, which know no law other than the insignificant urges of their own internal vitality, which is completely inexplicable? And when we look into human experience, the question is intensified because here we meet not only order and beauty but also the power to create both. The human ability to create purposive and meaningful forms, which appears to evoke positive responses not only in other human beings but even to some extent in the natural order itself, all that we sum up in the words 'civilization' and 'culture', this is surely among the most convincing indications of the teleological character of reality. Can human beings who embark on the creative enterprises which make life worth while deny this without denying the reality of their own most distinctive activities?

Of course, there is another side to the story, as those who argue against the teleological argument have been quick to point out. There is disorder, there is ugliness, there is much that appears utterly purposeless, there is death. The fact that these exist must engage our attention later on levels much deeper than those plumbed by the teleological argument. It is in its grappling with these that the special character of the Christian faith is most clearly revealed. The dys-teleological character of so much reality is certainly sufficiently strong to deny any clinching validity which this argument may claim and to prevent anyone from putting it forward with the complacency of Joseph Addison's hymn, 'The Spacious Firmament on High', as so many did in the eighteenth century. Here, at least, we have to stand alongside David Hume.[1]

Yet the fact that evidence brought forward to support a conclusion may prove inadequate to carry the full weight of that conclusion does not mean that it can then be dismissed as deserving no further consideration. Mr. Alasdair Macintyre has

[1] See N. K. Smith, *Hume's Dialogues concerning Natural Religion* (Edinburgh, 2nd. Edn. 1947).

made the point that the trouble with the traditional proofs for
the existence of God is simply that they are bad arguments.[1] If
that were all the trouble with them, nothing more would need
to be said. But is not part of the difficulty that, while they may
not be very good arguments, they do point to things which need
explanation and that the explanation traditionally offered is, at
least, sufficiently interesting to keep the conversation going?
Let it be agreed that it is theoretically possible that the world
may be a vast self-creating animal, as David Hume envisaged,
and that all its infinitely delicate and inspiring order and splen-
dour, so marvellously attuned as they are to our hearts and
minds, are its accidental by-products. It is possible, and the
teleological argument does not succeed in banishing the possibility. But is it likely? When Bertrand Russell says that the
argument from design is more palpably inadequate than any of
the others and has therefore acquired a popularity which they
have never achieved, it is fair to comment that he may again be
showing that lack of touch with the way in which the minds of
most men work which is often characteristic of very clever men
who may, perhaps, be excessively conscious of the way in which
their cleverness marks them off from their fellows. If it requires
the eye of faith to see that the heavens declare the glory of God
and that the firmament shows His handiwork, it requires an eye
darkened either by pride or folly not to see that there is glory in
the heavens and that the firmament shows someone or other's
extraordinarily busy handiwork, and that it is not easy for the
human spirit to rest until it can discover some meaning in this
mystery. And it may be just as much excessive pride in our own
powers and achievements as it is greater awareness of the in-
adequacies of the argument which prevents the men of this age
from saying as readily as their fellows in previous ages that it is
more likely that the order and beauty of life and the world
reflect the order and beauty of a Creator who is not ourselves
than that they have no significance at all except in so far as they
happen to take our fancy. The teleological argument provides
no proof of the existence of God. On its own terms, therefore,

[1] *Difficulties of Christian Belief* (S.C.M. Press, London), p. 65.

it breaks down. But by calling attention to order and beauty it enshrines a continuing challenge to those who assume that no God can exist or that no ultimate meaning need be searched for.[1]

Considerations of this kind become even more powerful when we recall the line of argument which came, in the nineteenth century, to have more authority than the traditional proofs, namely that which starts from the nature of our moral experience. When this received its first major formulation from Kant, it seemed to mark a great step forward because it shifted the argument from discussion of the nature of the external world to that of man himself. Two things seemed to be self-evidently true to Kant, the product of the Enlightenment and of Protestant piety, the starry heavens above and the moral law within. Of these, the latter had priority, and from it he was able to derive his three great postulates of God, freedom and immortality. That is to say, God was called in to justify the moral order. This was the road travelled, with various detours, by most of the philosophical theists of the nineteenth century.[2] Their faith has been, to quote the title of a famous series of Gifford lectures by A. E. Taylor which summed up this approach, the faith of a moralist.

It should be noted that among the powerful objections which have been brought against this line of argument in recent times there have been many which have been used by theologians. Is the moral law so self-evidently authoritative as Kant made it

---

[1] This is true even when we recognize the truth of the situation so eloquently described by Karl Heim in the introduction to *The Christian Faith and Natural Science* (S.C.M. Press, London, 1953, transl. of German original, 1949). The immense size of the universe and the range of time which it has passed through in order to reach its present stage intensify the mystery but, as Heim himself frequently points out, it does not invalidate the presence of order and design. It adds a vast new dimension to experience, a dimension which should prompt us further to humility and 'godly fear', but it is doubtful whether it involves a radical recasting of the terms of the discussion. To claim that would be to overlook the extent to which, before our time, men were aware of the great size of the universe and of the dys-teleological aspects of reality.

[2] See W. R. Sorley, *Moral Values and the Idea of God* (Cambridge U.P.).

out to be? In giving it such priority over all other factors in the human situation was 'the seer of Königsberg', like his numerous successors in Western Protestant lands, being unduly influenced by his own earnestness of temper, which was itself derived from a religious upbringing? Has not psychological study shown since Kant's day how much all men are conditioned, even in their formulation of moral ideals, by deep-seated instincts and urges over which they can achieve only very limited control? And has not anthropological study shown how relativized the expression of the moral law becomes when one moves from one culture to another? What place does belief in the self-evident authority of the moral law find for the kind of understanding we now have of the way in which ideologies, and utopias, are formed? And what significance in a world of morality is to be given to that radical evil whose presence Kant acknowledged towards the end of his life but for which he was unable to find any real place in his system? As the nineteenth century moved into the twentieth the threat which oppressed the spirits of many of its most profound and sensitive children was that of meaninglessness, which tempted some of them into nihilism. George Eliot was able to say to F. H. W. Myers that, as far as she was concerned, of God, immortality and duty, only duty remained.[1] But to those who were at a further remove from a sturdily Christian upbringing than she was, even duty itself began to relax its compulsive hold.[2] Those who find conviction in the moral argument appear generally to be those who still stand fairly close to the Christian tradition, at least in Western countries, even though they may have difficulties in being persuaded that revelation is able to vindicate its reality on its own terms. They are not often those who have come to a know-

[1] See Basil Willey, *Nineteenth Century Studies* (Chatto & Windus, London 1955), p. 204.

[2] It is true that Karl Heim is able to speak in *Christian Faith and Natural Science* of the emergence of a kind of nihilistic morality which emphasizes tolerance and fellow-feeling on the part of those who are caught in the human predicament. This appears to be not unlike the tolerance and courtesy so much commended by the latter-day Bertrand Russell. We are left with the question of how effective this passive morality can be.

ledge of God through moral experience alone. It is doubtful, therefore, whether it can be said that moral arguments can strictly be regarded as a form of natural theology.

Yet what was true in the case of the teleological argument is even more true here. The objections against arguments based on the character of moral experience are indeed formidable, yet the facts of the moral life remain, and they demand explanation with more urgency than do the less immediately practical considerations to which the other arguments call attention. Men everywhere have an awareness of right and wrong. The more highly developed they are, the more mature as human beings they become, the more intense, refined and normative of their conduct that awareness of right and wrong is. It is true that it finds widely differing expressions in different individuals, societies and ages and that, just because it is human, it is mixed up with all kinds of other things with which it is closely related and from which it cannot be easily isolated. Yet this awareness is always present and seems to be bound up with our awareness of our humanity itself. Even the most depraved ill-doer pays his testimony to the reality of the moral law, if only in his attempts to justify himself. In so far as people exist who appear to be practically a-moral they are normally considered to be deficient in an essential quality of humanity, to be more like animals than men. It is worth underlining the fact also that awareness of the reality of moral choice is related to the awareness of meaning and the enjoyment of significance of life in general. People have tried to live in our own time, free both of the burden of morality and of 'cosmic anxiety' and we have seen where it has led them. Edwin Muir described the summer population of St. Tropez in the 1920s in this way. 'Some years before, Aldous Huxley had described in *Antic Hay* the life of intellectuals in London who followed their inclinations. He made them vile, but the summer population of St. Tropez were merely lost in a featureless world which gave them too easy access to the satisfaction of their fleeting wishes; and those, being without meaning, remained beyond realization. They lived in an open landscape, without roads, or a stopping-place, or any point of the compass. Their brief love affairs resembled those of children who had acquired the knowledge and the desires of mature men and women, and in their conduct, and perhaps even in their thoughts, remained children. They were lost and on the road to greater loss, and ready to accept any creed which would pull their lives together and give them the enormous relief of finding, even under compulsion, a direction for their existence, whether it had a spiritual meaning or not.'[1]

There are ambiguities and even abysses in moral experience of which, largely ruled by convention as most of us are, we are only occasionally made aware. These warn us that we must not put our trust in our possession of moral consciousness and that there are further matters which need to be considered if we are to handle questions of morality aright. But the ordinary person is surely not misguided if he concludes, often enough even in the midst of his own moral failures, that his moral awareness is less likely to be a biological trick or a subtle piece of social conditioning than an adumbration of the will of a power beyond himself, to which he is answerable, and which upholds the right and condemns the wrong.

I should agree, therefore, with those who argue that neither the traditional proofs of God's existence nor arguments derived from moral experience are able to provide the foundation of a natural or rational theology which can usefully serve as a prolegomenon to a theology of revelation. But I should also want to maintain that they have value in a confused and half-believing world in helping to fasten the attention of men upon aspects of experience which call attention to the possibility of the existence of a God. Their cumulative effect in this respect is impressive even if it is not decisive.[2] Emil Brunner is unnecessarily trucu-

---

[1] Edwin Muir, *An Autobiography*, Hogarth Press, 1954, p. 229.

He goes on to say, 'There was something ambiguous in that life, for its freedom was not real freedom but the rejection of choice. Innocence and experience had intermingled in a way so simple that each spoke with the other's voice, and there was no grace in innocence and no virtue in experience.'

[2] See the summary in 'The Empirical Approach to Theism', Vol. II of *Philosophical Theology*, C.U.P., 1928, by F. R. Tennant.

lent, as his own handling of the matter itself proves, when he says outright that 'faith has no interest' in these proofs.[1] Paul Tillich has put the matter better, 'The arguments for the existence of God are neither arguments nor are they proofs of the existence of God. They are expressions of the *question* of God which is implied in human finitude. This is the sense in which theology must deal with these arguments, which are the solid body of any natural theology.'[2] We are sure that, especially in conversation with those who have drifted away from the dimension of mystery under the influence of scientific positivism, those who wish to raise the question of God may continue to find it useful to call attention to some of the considerations with which these arguments try to deal.

II

To say this, however, is to say only half, and the more positive half, of what needs to be said. If people were content to treat these proofs simply as 'expressions of the question of God which is implied in human finitude' matters would be relatively straightforward, but a great deal of the trouble in the history of theology has arisen from the fact that they have been determined to treat them as more. Banking on their validity as proofs, people have looked to them either to provide valuable supplementary assurance of God's reality to that given in revelation or, in some instances, even stronger assurance. People have, indeed, often been tempted to assume that the testimony of Christian revelation to God could only be accepted if, on other grounds, they were able to assure themselves that God really existed, misapplying the text, 'He that cometh to God must first believe that He is' by taking it out of the context of revelation in which it was spoken. This is the reverse of the Biblical contention, which it is the purpose of this book to maintain. It is because he sees this danger that Barth passes such severe strictures upon

[1] *Revelation and Reason* (English translation, S.C.M. Press, London), p. 340.
[2] *Systematic Theology*, Vol. I, p. 205.

natural theology. As ever, we could wish that he made a few more distinctions and qualifications, but no one has a surer instinct than Barth for detecting the presence of a real threat to the lordship of God and here he speaks with particular authority.[1]

From the point of view of trying to achieve a right understanding of the relation between revelation and reason, it is worth rehearsing again some of the objections to regarding the traditional proofs as means by which we come to a knowledge of God. The first is the obvious one that if these arguments are used as proofs rather than as pointers they lead us to a God who is very different from the Christian God, unless we have surreptitiously introduced an idea of God derived from Biblical revelation. Even when that happens, the Biblical idea of God is likely to become distorted in the process. Emil Brunner goes so far as to maintain that the 'God of the philosophers' is a rival of the Christian God and quotes frequently the saying of Pascal about 'the God of Abraham, Isaac and Jacob, not the god of the philosophers'. Here, like Barth, Brunner appears unduly influenced by a certain conception, derived largely from German university experience, of what a philosopher is like. One sometimes has the impression that what is set against the God of the philosophers is not in fact the God of Abraham, Isaac and Jacob but the God of the theologians, the natural rivals of the philosophers. As we have seen, it may be that we should give credit even to the idea of the absolute in Greek philosophy, an idea much spoken against by the theologians, for representing a much deeper insight *at the time* into the nature of what Godhead is like, hidden and revealed in Christ, than those which prevailed in the popular religions of the time. And in our own time, many philosophers have found it possible to discuss philosophical problems in a Christian way and even to be of not inconsiderable

---

[1] I am sure that Tillich would be prepared to agree with the need to qualify in this direction the quotation from him which we have made, as the context indicates. It is, perhaps, unfortunate that he did not go out of his way to do so if only to dispel the lingering suspicion in the minds of his readers that he is in danger of making 'the situation' almost as much a source of revelation as the Bible.

service to the theologians themselves, without setting up idols.[1] Nevertheless, philosophical speculation about God which is not checked and controlled at every point by what God has said about Himself in Christ is always in danger of leading men astray. God is made over into the image of men, even though they turn out to be very respectable men such as stern Scottish moralists or well-turned exponents of the perennial philosophy. The God reached by the way of the traditional proofs is so featureless that men cannot live with Him and the temptation to project into Him ideas of one's own becomes hard to resist. It is in this way that He becomes an idol.

It is a frequent charge against Thomist teaching that, although it sets out to make a sharp distinction between the spheres of revelation and of natural theology, it does not succeed in maintaining the distinction and allows its exposition of the nature and action of the God known in revelation to be coloured by a philosophy which is far from being the best vehicle through which to express it. The extraordinary discussion of predestination in the *Summa Theologica* which has no reference to the calling of God and the saving work of Christ at all is a striking case in point. In the same way, a great deal of the time and energy of recent Protestant theology has been taken up with trying to recover elements in the Biblical doctrine of God which had been lost sight of or distorted in the era when post-Kantian philosophy was dominating Protestant thought. To prove the existence of God, says Tillich, is impossible because God is one who lies beyond essence and existence. Existence is a derivative concept. Therefore, 'the ground of being cannot be found in the totality of beings nor can the ground of essence and existence participate in the disruptions and tensions characteristic of the transition from essence to existence.'[2] This is possible only

[1] See D. M. Mackinnon in *Essays in Christology for Karl Barth* (Lutterworth Press, London, 1956).

[2] See also Karl Heim, *Christian Faith and Natural Science*, p. 177. 'All inferences from the existence of the objective world to the basis of this existence, or from the purpose-serving structure of objective reality to a purpose-giving being which has produced it, lead always, so long as I leave myself out of

through the 'existential leap' which Christian believers call faith, the leap which, in its turn, becomes possible only because God has made available to men from beyond essence and existence the resources to make it possible. 'The god of the philosophers', who, as we say, is not necessarily the same as the God worshipped by all who undertake philosophical activity, is much more exposed to the danger of being a wish-fulfilment than the God of the Bible because a place has to be found for him where no place can be found since, by definition, he is a God who has not become incarnate in Jesus Christ.

Where these proofs are effective in buttressing real faith, as they sometimes appear to be, they are generally able to do this only for those who have been led to believe in God on other grounds. The Aristotelian proofs appeared to be convincing to medieval thinkers both because they accepted as valid the presuppositions of Aristotelian thought and because they were already convinced by Christian experience in the fellowship of the Church that God already existed. Their whole disposition was to look out upon the world for confirmation of that of whose truth they were already convinced. Similarly, as we have already partly seen, the moral arguments were clutched at eagerly by Protestants who were still anxious to insist that they knew God to exist and to be personal, just and loving, at a time of great intellectual change and confusion, when they were no longer confident of the ability of Christian faith to vindicate itself as true by its own inherent power. The corollary of this has been that those whose predisposition is not to believe in God's existence have always found it impossible to make the leap outside the causal system which they are invited to make by the cosmological argument. They have always insisted also on the dys-teleological aspects of the world as against the teleological argument and have always emphasized the relativ-

account, only to some still more remote cosmic cause, which must itself be the effect of some even more remote cause, and so on *ad infinitum*. Or else they lead to a general idea of God, such as might stand behind the whole, in other words to an entirely non-committal marginal concept which cannot be a source of strength to me in my practical life.'

ity and non-transcendental character of the moral law.

It is also not without significance that, despite the attempts of those who profess the 'perennial philosophy' to idealize the Tao,[1] the influence, both positive and negative, of natural theology has been largely confined to those Western lands which are the heirs of the Greek and Christian traditions. The fact that many people reject or fail to see the point of arguments is, of course, in itself no proof of their invalidity but it does suggest that more importance is given to those arguments than they can bear when they make little impact upon the minds of those who are trained to think in a different way, especially when great stress is laid upon their connection with the fundamental structure of the human mind by those who make them. The real trouble is that when prominence is given to 'natural theology', both the real grounds of objection to belief and the real grounds of assurance are in danger of being concealed.

When these proofs carry conviction what they do is, as Erich Frank has pointed out, to transpose the act of faith into the medium of philosophical thinking.[2] He goes on to make the point that the chief interest of the classical proof which we have not so far discussed, the ontological proof, is that it shows some recognition of this fact.

To see this may help to account for the curious status of this proof in the history of thought. When Anselm said in his Proslogion that if the idea of God was to be defined as that than which nothing greater can be conceived, God's existence must be included in the idea, since if He did not exist a being with the further perfection of existence would be greater than He,

[1] See C. S. Lewis, *The Abolition of Man* (Oxford University Press, 1945).

[2] Frank also reminds us that Thomas Aquinas said something which many of his followers appear to have forgotten when he prefaced his statement of the proofs of the divine existence in the *Summa Theologica* with the words 'Certain probable arguments must be advanced for the practice and help of the faithful but not for the conviction of the opponents, because the very insufficiency of the arguments would rather confirm them in their error if they thought we assented to the truth of faith on account of such weak reasonings.' Frank, op. cit., p. 46.

and hence God, many people have been understandably bewildered. They have protested that this is too simple, that such
an argument carries no conviction and that there must be a
logical flaw in it. As Kant observed, to have the idea of a hundred
guilders is not the same as having a hundred guilders in one's
pocket. In other words, conceptual knowledge is not the same
as existential knowledge. Yet at the same time, it has also been
sensed that, over-simple as the argument itself seems, the rebuttal
has also been over-simple. Somewhere, there is an overtone of
meaning which has been missed.

In our own time, more attention has been paid to the argument as it originally arose in the experience of Anselm, notably
by Karl Barth.[1] It has been pointed out that the argument arose,
not as a piece of general philosophical construction but as a result
of an insight given through prayer, prayer addressed to a God
in whom Anselm already firmly believed. The question which
Anselm is facing is a much more existential one, and a much
more characteristically modern one, than the form in which the
argument is couched, and than the title of 'ontological' which
has attached itself to it, might suggest. How can we be sure of
the existence of Someone who transcends everything we know,
even our capacity for thought? Can we ever disprove the assertion that God exists only in our imagination? This, as Frank
observes, might be taken as the beginning of the peculiarly
modern form of subjectivity. It is worth reminding ourselves
also, in view of the claim of this book that the most radical
questions concerning belief appear in the presence of faith itself,
that this question arose in the setting of prayer. It came between
Anselm and God in his prayers. Thought, in trying to transcend
the sphere of objective reality, is driven to realize its own
inescapable subjectivity and then is left with the problem of how
it knows its own concepts to be true. The difficulty fills Anselm
with despair, which indicates that Anselm sees that the God
whose reality he believes to be threatened is not merely a

---

[1] Anselm: *Fides Quaerens Intellectum*, English translation of 1960 of the
German first published in 1931, with a second edition in 1958 (S.C.M. Press
London).

possessor of existence, like other realities in the world, but the ground of all being. If He is unreal, there is no meaning. Anselm's despair, therefore, is literally existential. It is in his despair, when he casts himself on God, having no hope in his own powers of insight, that the illumination is given to him which produces his saying that God is the One than whom nothing greater can be conceived.

It is important to note that we are not told that this convinces Gaunilo. He continues to insist that Anselm is merely imagining the existence of God. The point is that Anselm himself, in the light of what he has now seen, no longer need fear that the atheist may be right. He knows that the God whom the atheist is denying is not the same God as the One whose lordship he has discovered anew in His revelation. What Anselm now sees and would like the atheist to see also, is that in the moment in which the atheist looks upon the idea of God as one produced simply by himself, he is no longer thinking of God, the Lord, the ground of being, but of something quite different, his own abstract idea, which is less than that than which nothing greater can be conceived. What Anselm's definition of God does, as Barth has pointed out, is to make clear what manner of God this is who is known in the act of faith in which the believer is enabled to rise beyond himself and his world. His argument convinces him only because he has known the transcendent God. He is the man of faith arguing on the basis of revelation. His prayer, which was answered, was that of *fides quaerens intellectum*, faith seeking understanding.

The question remains, however, as to whether this argument has any real value. Obviously, as a way of trying to convince the unbeliever of the truth of God it is, perhaps, the least effective of all the arguments. There is nothing in experience to which, on its own terms, the argument can appeal except the knowledge of God itself, which is what is in dispute. As a way of convincing the believer himself, it may appear merely tautologous, but it does have this important merit, at least in the form in which it came to Anselm. It is that it does pose the existential question concerning ultimate meaning and does call attention to the

lordship of God, His very Godhead, as the answer.[1] It avoids
the weakness of the other arguments, which is that they do not
pose the issues concerning God in the right way and therefore
encourage people to believe that they are facing them when
they are not doing so.

Life does not really pose the issues concerning the reality of
God in the way which is implied by those who would concentrate attention chiefly on the traditional proofs. The assumption
which they make is that we are able to reach conclusions about
ultimate issues by rationalistic means. The picture they present
is that of detached intelligences rigidly scrutinizing the evidence
with complete disinterestedness and honesty, trying, without
emotion, to discover whether it provides reasonable grounds to
justify God's existence or not. The truth, as we saw in the last
chapter, is normally very different. For the question concerning
the reality of God is not a problem, which can be examined, in
the way a mathematical problem can, by as near 'pure' reasoning
as men are able to get, any more than it is a merely 'interesting'
point of speculation which can be taken up or dropped according
to inclination without seriously affecting the thinker either way.
The question concerning God affects all parts of our being. The
nearer we come to the point of decision in relation to it, the
more anxious and involved we become and the more we find
ourselves fighting for our life.

The existentialist movement in philosophy has its full share
of the dangers to which all movements which arouse strong
attachments are open but its exposure of the limits of rationalism
may prove to be of permanent value. It makes clear that rationalism becomes irrational when it is maintained passionately as a
basic article of faith. It is not, in the ordinary use of the word,
'reasonable' to assert that you are dealing with a subject only in

---

[1] I am aware that this means that I am, in effect, saying that Anselm is
engaged in existential rather than ontological thinking in the customary sense.
Brunner observes that ontological thinking left to itself will always lead to an
idea of God which has more in common with pantheism than with the Christian
idea of God because it lacks the contrast between creator and creature (*Revelation
and Reason*, p. 345).

a cold, objective manner when it is manifest that you are doing nothing of the kind. The defect of rationalism is not its use of reason—that is its virtue—but its idolatry of reason, in which reason is not used but admired, and its reluctance to recognize the inescapable limits under which reason has to operate. This defect becomes calamitous when the most fundamental and far-reaching of questions, that of the existence of God, is under discussion.

We saw in the last chapter how necessary it is to scrutinize one's own motives in dealing with the grounds for belief in God because nothing is easier than to imagine that one is disinterestedly seeking the truth when one is, in fact, doing no more than seeking easy confirmation of a faith which is held without ultimate commitment or a justification for continuing in complacent disbelief. It is the weakness of the rationalistic approach that its method does not allow any place where the individual can turn round upon himself and examine critically his own motives. It does not take into account the 'life-situation' of the thinking subject, nor does its method provide him with 'candid friends' who, 'speaking the truth in love', can help him correct his bias. The result is that rationalism is always peculiarly exposed to the dangers of 'rationalization' when it tries to reach the level of ultimate meanings, because it cannot honestly face the dilemma in which men find themselves, that they cannot trust themselves to use the only instrument they possess for ascertaining truth, their reason, in a disinterested manner.

The word 'reason', of course, like the word 'faith' can be used in more than one sense, and this is a source of frequent confusion. The protagonists often pass and repass each other without ever meeting. For the purposes of our present discussion it is, at least, important to distinguish these two senses. The first is that of our capacity for reasoning, for putting two and two together and generally figuring things out. This we might call instrumental reason or what Tillich calls technical, as opposed to ontological, reason. Since human personality is a unity it works with imagination and intuition and the deeper and more complex the realities with which it tries to deal the more it depends upon these, but it is distinctive of it that it remains instrumental in character. We could, if we liked, call it morally neutral, except that, like all God-given distinctively human attributes, it possesses moral dignity and carries with it the obligation to function as worthily and efficiently as possible.

In view of misunderstandings which arise when these matters are discussed, it cannot be too strongly emphasized that there can be no permanent conflict between faith and reason in this sense. Man's possession of reason is one of his most vital, distinctive and noblest gifts. If to say that is to be a rationalist, we must all be rationalists. Any religion which sets aside reason in this sense or indeed fails to cherish and develop it is by that very act branded as a superstition. There can be no conflict between faith and this kind of reason, provided faith is genuine and reason is functioning properly, because faith must commend itself to and find appropriate fulfilment through the reasoning power of man if it is to register as true in his experience. And it must register as true because God desires truth in the inward parts. And it can only register as true, manifestly, by making sense to men's minds. They cannot, anyway, really accept nonsense. This must be true even in the presence of Tertullian's famous *Credo quia impossibile*. What he can only have meant is not that he really believes something because it possesses the chaotic and incoherent quality of the nonsensical but because he discovers in faith something which goes against his ordinary experience and which superficially appears to be more like nonsense than sense. When he finds that something which, to ordinary observation or even to the top of his own mind, seems to be nonsense still has the power of truth over him, he recognizes that the reason for this must be that, on a deeper level, it is not nonsense but that he has not yet been able to make the adjustments of understanding necessary before its truth and its exposure of the error of what normally passes for sense can become fully clear to him.

Any difficulties presented by the attempt to make truth presented by faith congruous with truth presented by other means, such as scientific knowledge for example, must be worked through by rational means to a rational conclusion. It is true that all the evidence must be taken into account and a too limited conception of what constitutes rationality sometimes prevents this from being done. It is true also that over some matters we may have to reach the sombre conclusion that the difficulties are too great for our limited intelligences to surmount and that we must learn to live with them as best we can. But even this conclusion, or especially this conclusion, must be reached by rational means and no one should pretend that it is anything but unsatisfactory. We may trust God who brings us so much light to retain His lordship over the darkness also, even though we may be unable to penetrate it, and yet recognize that we must continue to use His light, with our reason, to remove as much of the darkness as we possibly can. It is the nature of faith itself which demands this positive attitude to the use of reason on our part. The very fact that when God speaks, He speaks in His Word means that He wishes to address men in the most precise, intelligible and responsible mode of communication possible, through the use of language, that is to say rationally.[1]

It is only when reason is used in the second of our two senses that the familiar conflict between faith and reason begins to emerge. Here reason is used in what might be called a theological, or at least an existential sense.[2] It is the intellectual expression of the human will in self-assertion, the form taken by man's attempt to define himself to himself. It could be identified with self-consciousness, except that, in relation to faith, it is self-consciousness trying to define man's nature and ultimate destiny.

Christian belief maintains that men are sinful. This means that they resent God's right to be God and try to force Him out of His proper place in the universe and to set up themselves or an idol of their own creation in His stead. This causes the rift

---

[1] In view of many misunderstandings of his teaching on this matter, it should be said that Karl Barth constantly insists upon this point. See *Dogmatic*, I. 1, p. 231 and elsewhere.

[2] This, we suppose, is Tillich's 'ontological reason' but Tillich is unique in that he appears to be unable to be existential except through ontology. He cannot find the courage to live until he has first found 'the courage to be',

between the men they should be and the men they are which runs through human experience. The roots of this rebellion may be more traceable in the wills of men than in their reason but it affects their reason as well. Indeed, among those of reflective temper, whose wills find expression very clearly in their reason, this rebellion may find its most definite expression in their reason. They become subtle and adept, like the serpent in Eden, to find good reason to justify their rebellion and to savour their feeling of independence at the places where they are most conscious of themselves and of their power.

In fairness to Luther, it is essentially against reason in this sense that he directs his notorious diatribes, although it has to be admitted that he spoke with great violence and not always responsibly. He called reason a harlot, not because he despised man's reasoning power but because he had the insight to see that this noble instrument had been prostituted to serve man's spirit of proud self-assertion. Instead of fulfilling its true function of enabling men to glorify God through contemplation of His nature and discovering His will of truth and love in the world, it had become a weapon with which man attacked God.

When the challenge of faith confronts a man who is using his reason in this way, it inevitably comes as a stumbling-block. It appears to stand in opposition to reason because reason has now become the instrument of his sinful self-assertion. As Paul says, the Gospel comes as foolishness to those who are perishing. The Christian claim is that it is only when faith has done its transforming work in the citadel of his being that a man is able to see that what has happened is that the 'father of lies' has been cast out and that a right reason has been restored to him, which enables him to use his gift of rationality in harmony with the real nature of things. When it does that, however, its truth shines with such a blinding light that he is able to say, with the Hebrew hyperbole of Paul, that the very foolishness of God is wiser than the best wisdom of men. It needs to be seen with fresh conviction in these days that not the least of blessings which faith brings is that of intellectual emancipation and renewal.

The paradox of the situation is that this insight into the relation between faith and reason is visible only from within the experience of faith. It is another aspect of the paradox of Christian freedom, that we find freedom only in bond-service to Christ. It is this which makes the Christian faith so baffling, and often so irritating, to the person who believes that he stands outside the circle of faith and why it is certainly unhelpful for the believer to say to him that it is simply his sinful pride which prevents him from seeing it. That may indeed be true but he is not, by definition, in the position where he can see its truth and we are not likely to commend its truth to him by reiterating it truculently, under the illusion that in doing so we are genuinely confronting him with the stumbling-block of the cross. Nothing is a greater perversion of the classical Protestant understanding of the relation between faith and fundamental reason than to suppose that it encourages us, in P. T. Forsyth's memorable phrase, 'to fling the Gospel in people's faces in a Low-Church way'. We can only help the unbeliever to see that 'we speak God's wisdom in a mystery' by standing alongside him in his perplexity and making it our own and by helping him to see, in the way we have been made to see, how the coming of Christ does mean the restoration of a right reason by showing us how to deal with ourselves and each other and the world about us as nothing else does. Those who try to witness to the reality of faith must be particularly careful at present to avoid any suggestion that faith and irrationality have anything in common. Faith and unbelief are able to masquerade as each other very easily in this confused time and people are only too ready to accept clear-cut answers which have not taken account of the full range of the questions. We best vindicate the true rationality of faith by exercising our minds as honestly and courageously as possible upon asking the right questions and in refusing to accept any answers which do not commend themselves to our minds in the light of Christ.

This does not mean that, at the same time, we fail to recognize that in this matter more than any other, the initiative lies in the hands of God, who has His own ways, which are not necessarily ours, of commending His truth to men. We do not make faith acceptable to the unregenerate reason of man unless we identify ourselves with him in his intellectual struggles, but that is because we see him as he is, and our inseparable link with him, in the light of Christ. It is not because we can act on the assumption that there is a safe middle-ground on the fundamental level of experience where faith and unbelief can walk together as neutrals. As John Baillie says, 'Just as the unreality and impropriety of all arguments for the existence of other minds lies in the fact that they start from a possible solipsism, so the unreality and impropriety of the theistic arguments lie in the fact that they all start from a possible atheism. They start from a situation in which God is not yet. But there is no such situation, if it be true that in every moment I am called upon to obey His holy will—and that I have been so called from the beginning. Atheism is not a prior situation which theism must presuppose, but a situation which itself presupposes the theism of a world already challenged by the revelation of God in Christ.'[1] Otherwise, the issue between faith and unbelief need not be considered as one of fundamental importance.

The believer can best help the unbeliever not in this way but by asking him to reconsider his criterion of what constitutes rationality. This, after all, is the proper way in which faith begins its work. It makes a man look at his life in a new light and presents him with new experience which compels him to revise his judgments about himself and his neighbours. This is the reverse of undermining his proper confidence in rational thought and of driving him to take refuge in a flight from rationality which is then dignified with the name of a leap of faith. In this context, faith is best understood not as a leap into the dark but a leap into the light. Like the prodigal, the man of faith comes to himself and, like the man born blind, he now really sees. He is released to embark on the solid, rational task of giving order and coherence to what otherwise would relapse into chaos. Finding meaning in life, he is also able to impart meaning to it. A right reason has been restored within him.

[1] *Our Knowledge of God* (Oxford University Press), p. 176.

CHAPTER IV

The Exclusiveness of the Christian Claim to a Revelation of God

E ven if it be true that natural theology, as expressed through the rational 'proofs' of God's existence, has no more significance than that which we tried to give it in our last chapter, a large number of questions remain to be discussed. For there is not only philosophy in the world, there is also religion, which is infinitely more widespread in its variety and influence than philosophy. What significance must be attached to what the world's religions say about God or the gods and by what right do we Christians turn away from them and assert that the one true God has revealed Himself decisively only in the experience of the men of the Bible and of those who came after them?

Two very dissimilar factors have conspired, partly by their reaction upon each other, to prevent as thorough a discussion of these questions in Christian circles in recent times as their importance merits. The first has been that of theological liberalism. The temptation of liberal theologians in the early stages of the study of comparative religion, when horizons were expanding rapidly and men were learning a new sympathy with the religious aspirations of people of very different cultures from their own, was to understand the relations between Christian faith and other religions too easily and too superficially. The understanding of Christian faith itself which these theologians

had was often one which predisposed them to a certain syn-
cretism and when they also discovered that the heathen was not
quite as blind as their forefathers had supposed and that he did
not always bow down to stocks and stones, they were very ready
to say that Christianity and other religions were much nearer
each other than most Christians had been accustomed to believe.
The notion of 'progressive revelation' led these theologians to
say that God was always trying to reveal Himself to men and
that it was the way of Christian humility to recognize that He
had something to teach us about Himself through all religions,
and especially through the higher ones. Some went on to maintain that basically all religions were but different manifestations
of the one true God and that their adherents should co-operate
to learn more about Him and enjoy fellowship together through
their religion in His service.[1]

The critics of this approach have argued that it does not treat
with anything like seriousness the radical differences between
the world's religions. How can Hinduism and Judaism both be
right, at least from the point of view of Judaism? Are you
showing a proper respect for these religions when you minimize
their differences and say that, after all, what they are saying is
either the same or capable of harmonization with the rest? This
approach also asserts with far too great confidence where it can
see the hand of God at work in the world and overlooks what is
really distinctive in the Christian claim since it fails to see how
Christ's coming is intended as a judgment on all efforts of men
to rely on their religions as ways of reaching God. It represents
an anthologist's approach to religion, collecting 'other men's
flowers' but cutting them off from their roots and placing
them artistically in one's own environment without much
reference to the convictions of those who have produced
them.

The other factor which has helped to prevent adequate attention being given to these matters has been on a different side.
Theologians deeply convinced of the uniqueness and decisive-

[1] These ideas have found expression through such movements as the World
Congress of Faiths.

ness of Christian revelation have insisted that the only proper subject matter of theology is God as He is revealed through the Bible, summed up in Jesus Christ. To look for revelations of Him elsewhere is to dishonour God by disobeying the First Commandment. Karl Barth is, of course, the outstanding exponent of this point of view.

No one has a grasp of first principles in theology comparable to that of Barth and no one has done more to teach the Church what must be involved in accepting the fact that revelation has truly taken place in Christ. Yet his very grasp of first principles often seems to prompt him to lose interest in matters which may be less fundamental but which need a measure of clarification if our understanding of the first principles themselves is not to become confused. Even if the Christian has ultimately to reject what other revelations of God have to say about Him, he surely has an obligation to say why. And he cannot shut out the possibility that, in the light of revelation, God may be saying things of importance to him, as to other men, through these other religions. Surely, it is a dangerous form of theologism for the Christian theologian to assume that he knows what his relation to other religions should be before he has even troubled to enter into conversation with his fellow-men who follow them. The God who was in Christ makes clear the solidarity of all men in sin, including members of Israel, and also, as Barth himself has so magnificently demonstrated, their solidarity in standing under the promise of grace. This must surely mean that the Christian who is uninterested in conversation with his potential fellow-member of Christ who is a Muslim or Buddhist or animist and who is prepared to make confident generalizations about these other religions from his own limited and partial point of view, is open to the charge of the sin of pride. Lesslie Newbigin may well be right in saying that what provides the point of contact between Christian revelation and the men of other faiths is not their religion but their humanity,[1] but it follows from that very fact that we must show a human interest in their religion, if only with the humble sympathy of those

[1] *A Faith for this One World* (S.C.M., London, 1961).

who also know from their own experience how easy it is for men's religion to come between them and God.[1]

Strenuous efforts have been made more recently to make up for this lack of attention. Apart from anything else, the systematic attempts to consider the world-wide mission of the Church from a theological point of view, as notably at the Madras and Willingen conferences of the International Missionary Council, have inevitably focused attention upon the status of other religions and man's general religiousness. The unifying of the International Missionary Council and the World Council of Churches is also bound to mean that these questions will be still further explored, as they should be, as a major ecumenical concern of the whole Church. The revival of other religions, or at least their revived self-consciousness, has given a new urgency to the possibility of discussion with them in our increasingly unified world. Professor H. H. Kraemer and others have tried to give fresh accounts of the status of other religions from a Christian point of view, while the study of other religions, although still relatively neglected, has received fresh stimulus from the work of individual scholars and the work of American foundations in recent times.

The most commonly accepted and superficially the most attractive of the attempts to give an account of the pervasive religiousness of men is one which has received the blessing of Emil Brunner and other theologians. It is that there exists a general revelation of God in creation and history which reaches its fulfilment and finds its proper evaluation in the revelation in Christ. This notion has advantages over that of natural theology since it does not attempt to be a proof but a deduction from experience. It insists that the knowledge it provides is always distorted by sin and needs to be redeemed by Christ and has the

[1] As I have observed in my discussion of Barth's attitude to religion in *Beyond Religion*, Barth may be right in saying that the Yodoist Buddhism in Japan which is supposed to be astonishingly like Reformed Christianity cannot be the same as Christianity because it lacks Jesus Christ. But he surely cannot go on to assume because of this that all the other apparent resemblances are of no significance whatsoever.

further merit of trying to give some account of the reasons for the pervasive consciousness of religion among mankind.

The question which remains, however, is whether what this notion tries to account for is best described as 'general revelation'. We are left wondering whether it is really revelation and whether it is, in fact, general. Those who believe in a special revelation given in Christ are required to believe as a consequence of it that man lives out his life in the presence of God, *vor Gott* in Kierkegaard's phrase, whether he is conscious of God or not. His life, certainly his religious life, is best understood in terms of his reaction towards God. But is this situation one which can properly be described as one in which revelation occurs? Where does it lead men directly to the knowledge of the God whom we know in Christ? And is that knowledge in Christ true knowledge or not? Is not God veiled from men in their religious experience, even though it is true that they would not have religious experience unless they had been made for God and know no rest until they find their rest in Him? It is not an accident that they are always falling into idolatry, as Paul indicates in the famous passage in Romans I which is often taken as a Biblical justification both of natural theology and of general revelation.[1] The true God is present in the world and we ought to be able to discern Him, but the whole difficulty arises because we cannot and we cannot because we will not. Our sin prevents us from seeing God and our eyes have to be opened by faith before we can do so. If what we describe as general revelation were truly revelation, would special revelation be necessary? There cannot be real knowledge of God which is not personal

---

[1] The New English Bible certainly makes this passage sound like both, 'For all that may be known of God lies plain before their eyes; indeed God himself has disclosed it to them. His invisible attributes, that is to say his invisible power and deity, have been visible, ever since the world began, to the eye of reason, in the things he has made.' (Rom. i. 19, 20.) But Barth is not being guilty of special pleading when he argues that the Apostle is speaking here from the point of view of faith. His argument is that they ought to know God but they do not. It has to be admitted, however, that Paul is using a line of thought which is very similar to that used by many defenders of the idea of a general revelation through the Creation in our own day.

knowledge. But can we have personal knowledge of God without knowing Him as our loving Saviour, even when we know Him in His 'strange work' of judgment? Let it be agreed that the situation in which we find ourselves is one where man appears to be 'incurably religious'. He has an idea of God or of gods which finds a variety of expressions. He is fascinated by this idea but yet resists it. Of itself, however, it is unable to release him from the prison of his self-centredness. But is it not better to describe this as a state of estrangement from God by men made in the image of God in a world made by God whom they are unable, on their own resources, to recognize as God? And is it not better to reserve the word 'revelation' strictly for that action in which God Himself takes the personal initiative in revealing Himself to sinful men?[1]

Similarly, if this relationship to God which man has in virtue of his very humanity cannot properly be called 'revelation', can it any more properly be called 'general'? We realize that this is used to contrast it with 'special' but the word does imply that this knowledge is common to all men and consistent with itself. But is this so? There are, it is true, certain points of affinity between the teaching of some of the outstanding figures of the world's religions, although much more between its philosophers. But even these are a tiny minority of the whole and, in some instances, may have influenced each other, as in the case of the influence of the Bible on Mahomet. If Athens and Jerusalem have little to do with one another, Stonehenge and Benares have less. Is it possible, indeed, for the gods of both to exist in the same universe? It is the duty of the Christian to ask, humbly and with 'godly fear', what significance the various human religions have in the purpose of God, but what is the evidence which can

---

[1] It is not clear that, when he gets down to it, Brunner's understanding of 'general revelation' really amounts to any more than this. When he speaks of it as the same as Barth's conception of the *imago dei* in man, this certainly is the same as what we are saying. The *imago* can only be apprehended in faith. (*Dogmatic*, I, p. 135.) This is true even if we wish to invoke the Noachic as well as the Abrahamic covenant. Whatever status we give to this, it is a covenant of grace just as much as that is which was made with Abraham.

lead him to the conclusion that it is the same *general* revelation which speaks through them all. It is true that, as Joachim Wach, H. H. Farmer and others have shown, there is a certain structural unity in the religious experience of much of mankind. This unity is, however, extremely formal in character. As soon as its content in terms of the positive religions is examined, differences appear and the further one moves into each religious tradition, the differences appear to deepen. To describe all this, in its complexity, as 'general revelation', is to run the danger of creating an over-simplification which allows us to suppose that a difficulty has been removed when it has only been concealed under an impressive label.

The fact of human religion remains, however. What can usefully be said about in it a Christian context? This, at least, can be safely said from the limited point of view of the present inquiry. It is wrong to set about trying to work out the relation between Christian faith and the religions of mankind by surveying the whole field of religion in a comprehensive way, labelling its various types and then making some generalization about how these are related to Christian faith. Such surveys may be of value to help one get one's bearings in venturing into this vast field, but, as any good historian of religion will quickly point out, only as a preliminary to study, not as a means of providing the material for a Christian estimate of the significance of all the world's religions. The integrity both of the Christian faith and of the other religions would be gravely imperilled by such a procedure. There are several reasons why this should be so.

First, such a procedure underestimates so seriously the difficulty of entering into the world of thought and experience of other religions as to raise the suspicion that they are not being treated with proper respect, which is a fatal defect from a Christian point of view. The ideas of most religions are extremely hard for those whose minds have been formed in the Christian tradition to grasp, especially when Greek and scientific ways of looking at the world have mingled with the Christian. We spoke earlier of the difficulties which modern Western men often encounter in trying to understand the Christian faith,

The difficulties which confront them when they face Moham-
medan or Buddhist or Hindu religion, let alone primitive
religion, may be of another order, but they are certainly not
less. In fact a study of Western attitudes to these other faiths,
both positive and negative, would probably show even more
examples of dishonesty, impatience and self-righteousness than
a study of Western attitudes towards Christianity.

In the second place, all religions are obviously much more than
systems of ideas. They are ways of worship and they carry with
them distinctive attitudes towards living. Christians are always
protesting that it is impossible to understand Christian faith
without sharing in the worship and the common life of the
Church. This is certainly no less true of other religions, especially
when we recall how the affinity between their ideas and those
of 'secularized' modern Western man is much weaker than that
between Christianity and that man.

Thirdly, the real encounter between Christian faith and other
faiths does not take place on the level of generalized study at all,
except perhaps in the rare case of an individual scholar of unusual
imagination and power of identification. The ultimate reason
why we fasten our attention on the Christian revelation is not
because it happens to be the form of religion which is prevalent
in the society in which we live. It is because we believe that we
have met with the ultimate reality which, for want of a better
word, men call God in the life and work of Jesus Christ, and in
what led up to and has followed from that life and work. It is
our conviction that God has taken the initiative in addressing
men through Christ which determines our understanding of the
Christian faith and our approach to other religions. The question
of the relation of other religions to this faith does not present
itself with any urgency to us until we are met by the challenge
of that religion to our own faith, and that challenge is generally
most effectively expressed by believers in that religion. Renan
said in a famous phrase that in order properly to study a religion
it is necessary to have believed in it and to believe in it no longer
in any absolute way. Whatever we may think of the second part
of that statement, and it would need a great deal of elaboration

and discussion before it could be properly evaluated, it is undoubtedly necessary to have felt the breath of life move through a religion before one can honestly consider its significance for oneself. Christian faith does not simply confront Buddhism or Islam or religion in general. Christians meet Buddhists or Mohammedans, fellow-men whose view of life is radically different from their own. It is, therefore, the Christian missionary trying to reach people dominated by another religion or the man who is himself subject to the converting influence of another religion who is in the best position to evaluate the relation of that religion to his Christian faith. And the point at which this relation becomes a living issue in his experience will vary with the religion and the individuals concerned.

What must be emphasized is that to imagine that other religions can be neatly disposed of, maybe with a few generous and liberally-minded concessions, and then thought of no more is a dangerous form of complacency. It is on a par with the assumption that objections to the truth of the Christian faith which are not overtly religious can be dealt with in a preliminary 'apologetic' or 'philosophical' chapter, and that believers are free to talk about their faith as though objections did not arise at every step of the way for the theologian. The fact that other religions exist and that there are other possibilities before men which offer salvation can never be lost sight of by the Christian. The Bible itself, after all, is full of rivals to the true God and we are not given any assurance that those idols will be finally overthrown until the last. Indeed, we are told that it is a sign of the imminence of the End that false gods, such as the anti-Christ, will be particularly active. Why there should be other religions than that of Israel is part of the mystery of existence. Like the rest of the mystery, however, it must be accepted and no attempt made to wish it away, either by being over-positive or over-negative in relation to other religions. We cannot be so confident of our grasp of the truth that is in Christ that we can be sure beforehand what our relation to them should be, nor can we shut out the possibility that there is much to be learnt about God's purpose and our common human situation from them. Christian humility and the plain realities of the situation conspire, as usual, to prompt us to a cautious and empirical approach to this question.

We must remember also that Christian faith, and the faith of the old Israel before it, arose out of the soil of human religion, that its believers are exposed to similar temptations to those of other religious men and that the way in which the Spirit helps them to overcome these temptations throws light on their understanding of other religions. The experience of the men of the Bible themselves is of great importance here. It is curious how little attention is normally paid in modern discussions of the relation between Christian and other faiths to this fact, although Old Testament study emphasizes it very strongly.[1] The men of Israel were surrounded by and constantly influenced by other religions. They achieved their own distinctive faith in conflicts with those other faiths, sometimes conflict of the most direct and physical kind, as the story of Mount Carmel indicates. The religions they dealt with were different from those which confront us now and the situation in a world where Christ's Spirit is shed abroad is obviously not the same as that which the old Israel knew among the Canaanites.[2] Nevertheless, there are some conclusions which can be usefully drawn for our procedure today from Biblical experience.

The Bible is quite clear that the claims which other religions make upon their adherents must be repudiated. Whatever significance is to be given to them, they cannot be regarded either as revelations of God or as being in any sense on a level with Israel's God. Yahweh is a jealous God. He is truly the Lord, the final Reality, who cannot share His throne with another and who has entered into loving covenant with His people, who cannot be faithful to Him if they look in other directions. To

[1] See Von Rad, *Old Testament Theology*, Vol. I. English translation by D. G. M. Stalker (Oliver & Boyd, Edinburgh, 1962).

[2] Part of the difficulty with Barth's approach to this may lie in the fact that he sees the issues very much as Elijah did on Carmel. But Yodoist Buddhism is not Baal. What happens when the gods of other faiths remind us in some ways of Yahweh?

describe such activities the Old Testament uses a very ugly expression; it is 'to go a-whoring after strange gods'. Israel, which came into being only as a result of the Covenant, refuses to remain content with the joy of its Father's house but, like the prodigal, goes off in search of self-indulgent new experience. But the Bible also goes on to insist that the forces which lead men astray in the service of other religions are at work also in Israel. The elder brother who stays at home can betray God as much as the prodigal. Israel can be unfaithful to her Lord while claiming to keep the Covenant. It is Israel which finally crucifies Christ. This is the clinching proof that it is not our religion which saves us but only our God-given response to God's revelation of Himself. Part of the meaning of the work of Christ is that He takes human religion at its best and most representative, in the community of Israel, and shows that it cannot lead men to God.

It is because this is its message that we go to the Bible, without first trying to define our relation to the other religions of mankind in succession. We believe that we find here not merely the 'best religion' but also the divine judgment on the 'best religion'. The God of the Bible vindicates His reality both by calling into question the whole of man's religious quest and by providing him with the prize for which he has been searching in such a way that he has no basis for self-righteousness and God remains the Lord. This also is why we believe that, whatever truth there may turn out to be in other religions, it is truth which has to be checked and ratified by the God who has revealed Himself in Christ.

The reason for saying this is not that Christian faith encourages its practitioners in a dogmatic exclusiveness of temper. Christians often do show such a temper, and it is this which partly justifies the strictures of Arnold Toynbee and others against them. But when they do this, it is because they are displaying the characteristic sin of all men, a sin which becomes most obvious in the religious realm, where their deepest convictions are involved. With all due respect, the tolerant spirit of the Hindu religion, which Toynbee praises, is suspect here because it is a tolerance without commitment and without self-criticism. The believer in the Christian religion who goes and goes again to the foot of the Cross is made to see and to see again that God is not His possession but the King of all men, who judges and offers forgiveness to all men alike.

If it be protested that we have not answered directly the question whether other revelations of other gods may not be more true than the Christian one, it can be replied that the assertion about the nature of the finality we meet in Christ does partly answer it and also that the argument of the earlier part of this chapter must be recalled. Whether a true revelation of final reality has taken place can only be ascertained by giving heed to the testimony of those who have known that reality in their own tradition of religious experience. To try to discover this by a preliminary examination of religion in general is not possible. It can only be done by examining the claim of a particular faith to express and convey divine reality. It is to the examination of the Christian claim, as made known through the Bible, that we now turn.

CHAPTER V

God in Christ

For Christians, the answer to the question of belief in God turns on their answer to the question, 'what think ye of Christ?' In Him all the chief questions which arise in relation to belief in God are gathered up and brought to a decisive issue. It is true that there are many questions which might arise, especially in our minds today, with which He does not deal, those raised by modern science for example, and there are many others which He faced which need a good deal of translation before their relevance to our situation can be seen. At the same time, the fundamental issue concerning the reality of God is confronted so directly in the experience of Jesus Christ that we have to say that, if He is proved wrong, it is hard to see how belief in God as men have come to understand it under broadly Christian influence in the modern world can be sustained. I do not believe that, as many Western thinkers have supposed, it is possible to hold to a generalized philosophical theism while believing Jesus to have been mistaken in His central convictions. The argument of the rest of this chapter will try to make clear why this is so. If, on the other hand, He is right, this in its turn raises a large number of new issues which have to be faced.

Much of the work of theology has to be taken up with trying to discover and define the places where the central affirmations of faith are demanded and to distinguish them from secondary questions about which opinions might reasonably differ. Nowhere is it more important to do this than in trying to understand what Jesus Christ says, and does not say, about God. The meaning of His teaching, work and person, is, of course, the subject of endless discussion, and sometimes of debate, among His followers. But there are two points, important for our present purpose, which the vast majority would agree about. The first is that God, the final reality, Yahweh the God of Israel, was personally present in a unique way in Jesus Christ. The other is that what God revealed of Himself in Christ cannot be rightly evaluated except in the setting of the covenant which He made with His people Israel.

Jesus cannot be understood as an isolated figure of heroic proportions, who stands out from His background to such an extent that He becomes largely independent of it, and who compels attention by the quality of His personal magnetism and the weight of His individual authority. In so far as Jesus as a distinctive human being can be dissociated from the testimony to Him as the Son of God which surrounds Him, it is hard to form a clear picture of Him. The familiar liberal construction, or series of constructions, of the 'Jesus of history', helpful as they may be on some levels, conceal as much as they reveal. Although, as we shall emphasize again later, the reality of His humanity is made clear enough, Jesus himself was not interested, nor were His followers interested, in His 'personality'.[1] In a sense, they were not even interested in His message as an individual. Their concern was with the redefinition of the vocation of Israel and the function which He performed in the fulfilment of that redefined vocation. Men came to know Jesus as He challenged them and changed their lives. They knew Him through His benefits, to echo Melanchthon's familiar phrase. Those benefits were reconciliation and communion with God, a new understanding of His will and a new ability to fulfil that will. It was because of these that they asked 'What manner of man is this?' and it was in the light of the redefinition of God's covenant with His people that they gave their answer that He was the Christ, the son of the living God.

[1] This is a modern corruption and vulgarization of the ancient idea of the 'soul'.

God in Christ

There is no necessity, at this point, to attempt to give a comprehensive account of Biblical teaching about God, but it is worth reminding ourselves how germane to our discussion that teaching is. Like most other disciplines in modern times, theology suffers in its own way from the vices of over-specialization and discussion of belief in God has undoubtedly suffered from the unspoken assumption that, somehow, grounds must be discovered for accepting the Biblical evidence which are other than those provided by the evidence itself. Likewise, even when Jesus' experience of God is taken into account, as it inevitably must be in any extended treatment of the subject, that experience is not always clearly enough related to what has gone before it in the Old Testament. This does not happen among Biblical theologians in these days, since Hoskyns and Lightfoot, and now Von Rad, but it does still tend to happen among many systematic theologians and Christian philosophers.

Roman Catholic theology in particular is at fault in this respect, as an otherwise notably illuminating book such as Karl Adam's *The Son of God* demonstrates. The Biblical evidence is more commonly not given its due weight, however, because of the prevalence of the familiar modern attitude which is over-impressed with the novelty of the difficulties in the way of faith with which it is confronted and which lacks the historical sympathy to appreciate how similar many of them are to those with which the men of the Bible had to deal. The fact remains that no one can undertake a realistic discussion of what belief in the Christian God means without devoting not merely a part but the major part of his attention to the Biblical testimony about God, which reaches its culmination in Jesus Christ.

This testimony is misunderstood unless two points which have already been mentioned are borne clearly in mind. The first is the extent of the Biblical awareness of mystery, both in relation to God and to human existence, and the other is the necessity of making an effort always to look at the Biblical material with fresh eyes and in its proper historical context. Where this does not happen, the Bible is approached in a two-dimensional way, in terms entirely of subject-object relationships, which prevents the question of God arising at all in an existential way, however often the word 'God' may be used. The recovery of a genuinely historical approach to the Bible, which is what the researches of nineteenth-century critics, and those who came after them, made possible, has been of great assistance to the Church in recovering its understanding of the uniqueness and sharpness of revelation.

A very good illustration of this, and of the difference between what we call a two-dimensional and a three-dimensional approach to Biblical revelation, is provided by the different attitudes which they produce to the traditional arguments in support of revelation derived from miracle and prophecy. If these are put forward as bare facts, they carry little conviction. The men of the nineteenth century did right to react against them on this basis, and it is understandable that they should seem to men of scientific temper who are encouraged to think of them in similar terms to be obstacles in the way of arriving at faith rather than as confirmations of its truth. But they were not formulated in this way in the first place. They were attempts, broken and fallible as all such attempts are, on the part of men who were caught in events greater than their understandings could fully comprehend, to express their insight into a purpose which moved according to a law different from and more fundamental than that of earthly appearance, the law of a God whose thoughts are not as our thoughts nor His way as our ways.[1] Prophecy implied discernment of the divine logic in events and its fulfilment represented confirmation in later experience of what those who had gone before had really but imperfectly apprehended. The community of experience between those who prophesied and those who were able to recognize the fulfilment of prophecy was an indication that the same divine purpose was at work in both. Miracle, in the sense not of an isolated unusual event which goes contrary to the normal work-

[1] See Tillich's characteristically sensitive and illuminating discussion of 'miracle' and 'ecstasy' in *Systematic Theology*, Vol. I. We have to add that they are not, perhaps, as helpful as they might be because, also characteristically, they are not directly enough related to the Biblical material.

ing of nature but of a sign in the natural order of the presence
of divine reality in the realm of personal encounter, only derives
its significance from the fact that it leads on to an intensive
apprehension of the divine action. Both need to be thought of as
moving in the dimension of mystery and of requiring an attitude
of wonder on the part of the person trying to understand them.
This may not remove all our difficulties in relation to them but,
at least, it helps us to see how they can become confirmations
of the divine reality rather than hindrances to our apprehension
of it.

The mysterious character of the Biblical testimony is concealed to some extent by the way in which the Bible opens. It
begins with an apparently factual account of the creation of the
world and man, together with a story describing the life of the
first human beings and the origin of sin. This naturally encourages those of rationalistic temper with a 'two-dimensional'
attitude to assume that this is typical of the whole Biblical
approach. One of the earliest and solidest achievements of careful critical study of the Biblical documents has been to show that
it is a misinterpretation of these early stories to treat them as
factual accounts of historical events. They are a recasting of
ancient myths of creation, paradise and the fall of man, produced at comparatively late stages in the history of Israel, and
reflecting a highly-developed understanding of a God who had
already entered into personal dealings with His people through
the Covenant and the Law. This does not, of course, detract
from the authority and insight of these stories; it adds to them,
but in a different and profounder way. They are now seen, not
as divinely transmitted accounts of external events, presented in
a form which lends itself to scientific verification, but as a
speculative interpretation, in the light of a knowledge of God's
transcendent purpose derived from another source, of how a
universal human situation has come into existence. These stories
are not deductions from a 'general revelation' given in the
creation. They are imaginative expressions of permanent realities, with which other religions have also tried in their own way
to grapple, but now illumined and given meaning by the

knowledge of God's purpose made known in His covenant with Israel.

The element of mystery is much more clearly present in the first part of the Bible of major importance which bears some relation, however hard it may be precisely to determine the nature of the relationship, to historical fact. Once again, there may well be significance in this fact, that the element of mystery becomes more and not less pronounced the nearer we approach the historical. The covenant with Abraham appears to have its beginning in the most enigmatic manner possible. He is suddenly confronted by Another, who tells him to leave his home and family and friends and simply to trust the Other. (Genesis xii. 1–2.) On the face of it, Abraham's acceptance of this prompting might seem to be no more than one of those lucky chances of which life is made up, providing evidence of the capriciousness of the forces in control of human affairs rather than of any continuous purpose. But that what confronted Abraham is no mere epiphenomenon but a Reality who is unique in human experience is proved not merely by the giving of the Covenant, which might in itself be no more than a way of conferring dignity upon the origins of a particular nation, but by the amazing story of the sacrifice of Isaac, which follows on immediately from the giving of the Covenant.

To try, at this time of day, to discover what is history and what interpretation in the story of Abraham and Isaac is beyond human capacity. The story is clearly parabolic in intention. What does stand out beyond any shadow of doubt is that no one can have written that story, in that particular context, who did not have personal dealings with the same Reality as was present in Jesus Christ.

The story is unintelligible except against the background of the Covenant. As we have seen, on the face of it the idea of the Covenant might seem to be yet another example of the way in which nations like to give impressive accounts of their origins and of their 'manifest destiny' were it not for the quite extraordinary way in which the Covenant is ratified and its promise fulfilled in the experience of Abraham. First, it bears fruit only when Sarah is long past the natural age for the bearing of children. This means that its fulfilment is to owe nothing to Abraham's natural vitality or to the virtue of the stock of Israel. Abraham is indeed to be justified only by faith. Secondly, Isaac is born in this miraculous way in Abraham's own old age. He loves Isaac the more because he has come when all hope seemed to be gone. 'And Isaac spake unto Abraham his father, and said, My father; and he said, Here am I, my son.' Yet it is this Isaac whom God asks Abraham to offer up in sacrifice. That is to say, God demands that, in obedience to Him, Abraham destroys the one through whom alone, humanly speaking, the covenant can be fulfilled. Yet, with supreme insight, he sees that, greatly as he loves Isaac, to love him more than God is to fail to see the point of the covenant of which Isaac is the precious fruit. It is only when he raises the knife to slay Isaac that he is in a position truly to carry on the covenant and that it becomes possible for Isaac to be God's servant. Abraham has understood what the lordship of God means. The Christian imagination has rightly seen the ram caught in a thicket as a pre-figuration of Christ and the relation between Abraham and Isaac as that between believers and the Church. Here, at the outset of the story, miracle and prophecy contrive to point to the truth which the teaching and death of Jesus Christ finally exemplify that this God can only be served by those who are prepared to die that they might live. From this moment onwards, it is clear that a unique power is at work in human affairs.

The same mysterious reality, hidden and revealed, is at work in the other determinative events of the Old Testament, shining forth from their setting in the general religious experience of men in Israel and in the other nations with whom Israel was in contact and through all the misunderstandings and corruptions of her vocation of which Israel was guilty. It is typified in the great story of the third chapter of Exodus, where the sublime sign of the burning, unconsumed bush causes Moses to turn aside to see, to penetrate the dimension of mystery, and there to receive Yahweh's Word of redemptive compassion for His people. This Word receives its fulfilment in the great paradigmatic experience of the old Israel, the miraculous Exodus, which is further differentiated from an event for which a purely naturalistic explanation might be possible by the giving of the Law on Sinai, an event which is recorded in such a way as to give an overwhelming impression of the otherness and majesty of God, and which sets Israel on a road which marks her out decisively from all the other peoples of the earth.

That the Church has not been fanciful in seeing the hand of the same God as she knows in Christ at work in the patriarchal narratives and in the Exodus is proved by the nature of the body of experience which provides the main link between the Church and the God of Abraham, Isaac and Jacob, that of the prophetic tradition. This tradition finds expression not only in the great prophets of Israel, from Elijah and his precursors onwards, and in the worship which gathered round the Temple, particularly as it found expression in the Psalter, but also in such writings as those of Job and Jonah. The significance which this remarkable body of experience has for the question of the truth or otherwise of belief in the Christian God has not received the attention it deserves because of the difficulty we have today in seeing denials and affirmations of God's reality in any other terms than those to which we have become accustomed.

A very good example of this difficulty is provided by the attitude of Martin Buber, although the matter is complicated here because he is writing from a Jewish point of view and criticizing Christian ideas. Despite his great personal authority on these matters, it is hard to believe that he is right when he says, in his book *Two Types of Faith*, that there is no denial of the existence of God in the Old Testament. This can be true only if the most abstract Greek connotation be given to the term 'the existence of God'. He makes a distinction between *diurnal*, trust, and *pistis*, faith, saying that the one is characteristic of the Old Testament and the other of the New. *Pistis* came into Hellenistic Judaism through Paul. It is a conviction that the God whom one cannot see is there, a demonstration, a proof of His existence. But, as Buber says, 'To the man of ancient Israel such a proof is quite foreign, because the idea of the nonexistence of God lies outside the realm of that which was conceivable by him. He is made to see (Deut. iv. 35) that the God of Israel, "his" God (vii. 9) is not a special God but the only God, and nevertheless also the "faithful" God to whom he may entrust himself; that there is "a" God, he "sees" apart from this. Even when it is recorded of the "transgressors" that they deny God, it means that they presume God not to be present, not to care about the affairs of the earth. Whether this man recognizes God's rule or objects to it, whether he is responsive or refractory, he lives by the fact that God is, no matter how he lives.'[1]

In all this, Buber seems to contradict his own type of existentialism, perhaps in the interests of the sharp anti-Paulinism of the book as a whole. Whatever may have been its usage in Hellenistic Greek, it is absurd to describe *pistis* as Paul used it as a word meaning assent to a formal proposition. Where does this stand in relation to Paul's so-called 'faith-mysticism' in relation to Christ? When he speaks of the faith which justifies, he is never speaking speculatively. He is speaking of the act of personal commitment to God as revealed, a God whom he 'sees' to be 'faithful' in the way Abraham and Moses did. The truth is that Buber does not seem to understand what Paul, and the Reformers, meant by justifying faith, despite the fact that he himself has helped us so much to understand the personal dimension in which the meeting which evokes faith must take place. By the same token, can it really be maintained that the Old Testament takes God for granted in the way he suggests? It is true that the kind of overt denial of the existence of God which is found in the modern world, and which was also partly characteristic of the Greek world which influenced that of the New Testament and the later Old Testament, is not typical of the Old Testament as a whole. But surely, when men denied the relevance of God and doubted His power, that was their way of denying His reality. Their implication was that Yahweh was not really Yahweh, the Lord, but only one god among others, whose

---

[1] *Two Types of Faith* (Routledge & Kegan Paul, London), pp. 37–8. See also, for a criticism of Buber, Emil Brunner, *Dogmatics*, Vol. III (Lutterworth Press, London) pp. 159–62.

existence they could safely ignore or treat as of secondary importance. 'How doth God know? And is their knowledge in
the most High? Behold, those are the ungodly, who prosper in
the world; they increase in riches.' (Psalm lxxiii. 11–12.) The
Hebrews, like the French, were a practical people, who thought
in very concrete terms. They also had a vivid awareness of the
majesty, moral power and ceaseless activity of God in relation
to human affairs. To say that this God could be ignored or defied
with impunity and that the way to get rich was to be ungodly
was as direct a way of saying that God, the Lord, did not exist
as their minds were able to achieve. Their attitude to God is
more immediate, both in affirmation and denial, than that expressed in the Pauline *pistis*, but this is because Paul is trying to
grapple with that rift in personality, sin, the power behind unbelief which prevents us from thinking straight, which led him
to believe in Christ as mediator between the hidden God and
man. It is not without significance in this context that Buber
does not deal with what faith means in relation to Christ and is
able to claim Jesus simply as a great Jewish teacher, without
considering what the cross and resurrection mean. But if unbelief means disobedience, turning one's back upon God, there can
be no question that unbelief is to be found in the Old Testament.

Indeed, I am prepared to maintain that the encounters between prophets and people in Israel are among the classic
examples of faith and unbelief in action against each other, and
that they throw a great deal of light on our understanding of
the relation between them at the present time. The prophets
speak in the name of a God who stands over against Israel and
is in no sense to be identified with her. He is One who, as Amos
makes clear, Israel would often prefer to forget and whom she
tries to render innocuous through the performance of acts of
ritual obedience which do not involve radical commitment. But
the prophets will have none of it. His promise is only given to
those who are conformed to His holy will, as Isaiah insisted.
Only those who are prepared to act on this, who are God's
servants, can be accounted as true members of Israel. Of nothing
are the prophets more conscious than of the intractability of

God in the face of human attempts to manipulate Him. He drives them to prophesy when they would prefer to keep silent. They wrestle with Him, as Jeremiah does, to try to avoid His burden and discover, as the 139th Psalm does, that there is no escape from His constraint. Whatever else the record of the great prophets of Israel conveys, it conveys an overwhelming sense that they were dealing with a transcendent Reality, in whose presence any wishful thinking was ruthlessly exposed and rejected.

The superficiality of the statement that the old Israel did not envisage the possibility of the denial of God's existence is further underlined by this very fact that the Word of the Lord came to them so often as a word of judgment. It is not true of any men that they reach intellectual conviction about God's reality first and, only when that is established, move on to consider the ethical implications of this belief. It is peculiarly untrue of the people of Israel, who thought in very concrete and realistic terms. They knew God through His actions. The prophets were very articulate, but they nearly always tried to point out the hand of God at work in the great events which determined the corporate destiny of the people. Just as God indicated His reality by His actions, so His people showed their unbelief by their disobedience. The call to repentance and the reminder that the day of the Lord was at hand, which was the most characteristic message of the prophets, was a reaffirmation of the divine reality. It was an assurance that God still reigned, that His purpose was going inexorably forward and that, whether they liked it or not, His people were answerable to Him. Perhaps the most remarkable feature of the whole prophetic witness in Israel, and the surest indication that it truly points forward to Christ, is the complete refusal of the prophets to be taken in by professions of devotion on Israel's part. They are positively cynical about them. Israel's religion was not enough to save her. Only the loving-kindness and the power of her Lord could do that and the condition of their doing so was her recognition that the will of God was not to be identified with the will of Israel. Israel has to be led through her religion to the final crisis, in which she stands naked and empty-handed before the judgment and promise of her Lord.

It is only when Israel has done this that guidance is given her for the future and that the Covenant is carried forward. Here again, we see how a right understanding of prophecy helps us to understand the meaning of revelation. The point of the prophetic witness lay not, of course, in the ability of the prophets crudely to foretell the future in terms of external events nor even that they were able to 'forth-tell' what was likely to happen, in the sense of having such a grip on moral realities that they were able to forecast intelligently the course of events if Israel refused to follow what they advocated. It was that when they recalled Israel to her true relationship with God and led her into the situation where she submitted herself to the judgment of God, her faithful servants received forgiveness and guidance for the next step of the way. All this took place in the midst of the ambiguity and confusion which are characteristic of human affairs. Because of Israel's disobedience, the prophetic witness became more and more of a 'minority report'. The line which led to Christ was carried forward by a remnant and the fulfilment of the promise was projected forward to a Day of the Lord which would come to pass in God's time and on His initiative rather than through anything done by the empirical Israel. Nevertheless, through all this, the purpose does go forward until the climax is reached in the coming of Jesus Christ.

II

Nothing has received more attention in the course of Christian history, for obvious reasons, than the meaning of the person and work of Jesus Christ. As we have already emphasized, however, it has not always been sufficiently appreciated how much our attitude towards the question of the reality of God is bound up not only with our evaluation of that person and work but with Jesus' own attitude to that question. The whole discussion of the reason for the existence of God in Christian history has suffered because primacy has not been given to Jesus' own experience of God as He himself interpreted it and as that worked out in His own life and in what issued from that life. One of the many merits of the Christocentricism of Barth and those who follow him is that it has brought Jesus into the centre of the picture when we consider this matter, although even here Barth's impatience with trying to explain and justify the ways in which his procedure differs from those customary in other theological circles has prevented many people from seeing all the implications of this for belief in God. It shows a radical misunderstanding of the person and work of Jesus Christ, and of the critical rather than merely expository method which theology must use, to assume that the question concerning God's reality precedes that of our attitude to Jesus Christ. Our answer to the question 'What think ye of Christ' is not determined by our answer to the prior question, 'Do you believe there is a God?' The evidence provided by Jesus himself is our chief source for making up our minds whether God exists or not. Or if this is, as Barth would rightly remind us, the wrong way to put the question, it is the evidence provided by Jesus Christ Himself which makes us see how and why it is wrong. Unless this is seen, the question is improperly posed from the outset.

The first point to note in speaking of a revelation of God through Jesus Christ is that the setting in which the account of this life is placed must not be allowed to conceal from us the fact that it started from our common human situation and that the conclusion of His divinity was reached slowly, cautiously and with reserve. The more developed accounts of His work and person which we have in the New Testament itself speak with great boldness and richness and finally see Him as the Pantokrator, the Lord of all created things, 'whose fullness filleth all in all.' But such passages as the first chapters of Hebrews, Colossians and Ephesians, and for that matter, the prologue to the Fourth Gospel, represent the fulfilment rather than the beginning of the story. The nativity stories in Luke were written after the event and in the light of its fulfilment and it was only after the Spirit had enlightened their eyes that men knew that,

when Jesus was among them, it was the grace and truth of the
only-begotten of the Father that they had seen.

We are not, for example, given any kind of reason why Jesus
should have appeared at that particular point in history rather
than at any other. 'In the fulness of time', Paul said, 'God sent
His Son', but it is not made clear why, according to our human
computation, this rather than any other was the fullness of the
times. Indeed, as far as we can see, this was not necessarily a
more appropriate time than many others in history for the
appearance of God's unique revelation. Pious Christian reflection
has tried to show that the time was ripe because Israel was now
part of the Roman Empire. This had drawn the ancient world
together and opened up Western Europe to the possibility of
influence from the Near and Middle East for the first time,
while Greek ideas and language provided a widely understood
universe of discourse. It is doubtful, however, whether these
considerations, even if accepted at their face value, are sufficient
to justify us in believing that we can see why this was 'the fulness
of time'. Even in the internal history of Israel, which was an
extremely small segment of world history, the great prophets
had long since passed away and several centuries of relative
mediocrity had intervened. At the time when Jesus appeared,
there was a great deal of restlessness, uneasiness and expectation
but it is not clear that it was any greater than at several other
times. And when the situation of the rest of mankind is taken
into account—the Chinese and the inhabitants of the American
continent, for example—the mystery becomes unfathomable.

The terse, abrupt opening of St. Mark indicates what the
right attitude is here. 'The beginning of the Gospel of Jesus
Christ, the Son of God.' There is no point in speculating why
Jesus appeared at that moment rather than any other in the
confused, enigmatic and often irrational course of sin-twisted
history. It is enough that He came and that He set about doing
for man as a man what only God could do. What the apparent
contingency of the coming of Jesus underlines is that He was a
man, who partook to the full of the mutability and particularity
of human existence.

This needs to be dwelt upon, because it is of the utmost importance in trying to understand the way in which the evidence of Jesus for God's reality is significant for us. Whatever else Jesus was, we must start from the fact that He was a man as we are. We do not reach His humanity through His divinity but His divinity through His humanity. A good deal of the trouble with ancient orthodoxy, especially in the East, and of the churches dominated by ancient orthodoxy, is that, although there was no reason why this should be so, they started with His divinity. The attempt to recover 'the Jesus of history' of nineteenth-century scholarship may not have been very successful because they approached His humanity with too many romantic preconceptions and because they sometimes tried to drive a wedge between the Jesus of history and the Christ of apostolic faith, but they have done a great service in making us realize that it is through our knowledge of His humanity that we are faced with the question concerning His divinity.

To say that Jesus was fully a man is, of course, to say no more than what the Creeds and the classic confessions of Christendom have always said but the full impact of that fact has not always been made upon Christian thought and Christian devotion when they may have moved away from the living springs of faith. It means that Jesus' life, in His coming into being and in the way in which His ordinary human experience developed, was exposed to the same fortuitousness as that which belongs to the lives of all mortal men. Whatever may be our view of the status of the doctrine of the Virgin Birth, it must always be a point for discussion as to how far it is compatible with accepting the full humanity of Jesus, if only because to be a man means to be born 'of the will of man' as well as of God. He also accepted the inevitable limitations which are involved in being a man. He had no more physical power, no greater knowledge of human history and no more experience of ordinary life than can be held within the span of one man's comprehension. Even when He performed what His followers took to be miracles, they were such as one man could perform, works of healing and compassion which required a personal contact or mediation.

His Spirit was not yet shed abroad, moving with the freedom of wind. His obedience to God had to be accomplished, in terms of human possibilities, with the same resources and in the face of the same obstacles as confronted other men. Above all, what knowledge of God He possessed came to Him through the same channels as it did to other men and had to overcome the same resistance of misunderstanding and doubt. In the light of His finished work, His followers see all this to have been a voluntary self-limitation, but that does not alter the fact that when He lived as a man among men the limitation under which He existed was a real one.

The consequences of this for our inquiry are clearly of the first magnitude. For it means that the question concerning God's reality as well as His nature must have posed itself in the same terms for Jesus as it does for any other man. Or if the terms vary according to differing historical situations, the question is the same question. It is for this reason that we say that the answer of Jesus to that question, and the honouring by God of that answer, is of decisive importance. As we have seen, men tend to assume that Jesus has to justify His belief in God at the bar of human judgment which is somehow in a better position than Jesus to know whether God exists because Jesus is 'automatically' on the side of God. But if Jesus was truly a man, there was nothing automatic about his being on the side of God. He was the representative of Israel, and the word 'Israel' means 'the contender with God'. Doubt of the validity of His calling and misunderstanding of its nature were present realities in His experience and He had to fight His way through them as other men have to. When He reached faith, He reached it in the same way as other men do. It is true that, like the men of the Old Testament in whose succession He stood, the possibility of unbelief presented itself to Him in terms of doubts concerning God's purpose and His own calling but it is more directly true of Him than of any other man that this was a concrete and realistic way of facing the question of God's saving reality. His whole ministry is worked out in terms of a conflict with the power which is present in unbelief. The Gospel is the story of the triumph of grace against unbelief in the experience of men. This is why it is the faith of Jesus which challenges the unbelief of men rather than the other way round.

This could not be made clearer than it is in the wonderful story of the Temptations, which is placed, in formal and deliberate manner, at the very beginning of Jesus' public ministry in St. Matthew. This is much more than an attempt to consider and to reject various inadequate ways of fulfilling His calling from God. It is a testing, a proving of the faith of Jesus, of the kind which He asks his followers to pray to be spared,[1] an intense struggle in which the reality of His vocation and, therefore, of the God who has called Him, is radically challenged.[2] The stylized placing of one citation from Scripture against another by Jesus and Satan does not mean that this was an academic exercise, a sham fight. On the contrary, it meant that the temptations presented themselves in the first place as the will of God and that it was only through deeper pondering upon the meaning of God's covenant with Israel that He came to see that they were in fact ways in which God was denied. Religion is the greatest enemy of faith. It is the devil who is the most skilful quoter of Scripture and the most eloquent preacher. It required the utmost critical vigilance on the part of Jesus in His humanity to detect what was wrong in the apparently public-spirited and reasonable possibilities which were put before Him in the first and second temptations and to see that they ultimately involved putting himself, and therefore Satan, in the place of God.

This becomes most obvious when we consider the last and strongest of the temptations. This is often taken to mean that Jesus was faced with the possibility of using His great gifts of leadership in order to establish His political domination over mankind. This must certainly be part of the meaning. Jesus' repeated reminders to His disciples that they must be humble

---

[1] Matt. vi. 13.

[2] *Dubitare* contains the same root—that of the adjectival numeral *duo*, two— as *duellum*, a struggle. Doubt, Pascallian doubt, agonistic or polemical, rather than the systematic doubt of Descartes, presupposes the duality of combat.— Unamuno, *The Agony of Christianity*, p. 27 (Payson & Clarke, N.Y., 1928).

and that leadership must be exercised, not by lording it over the flock but by taking the form of a servant, shows how much He was aware of the persistent strength of this temptation to all who have the opportunity to exert influence over their fellow-men. But the temptation is more comprehensive than that. Like all the temptations, its primary reference was to Jesus' relation with God and how that was to be interpreted. It was an on-slaught of unbelief. And we can be confident that it is most fully understood as the equivalent in His terms of the tempta-tion which comes to us today in the paler, more academic form of humanism.

Jesus was a man. He was also, as men go, a very great man, one of unrivalled insight, balance, gift of expression and moral authority. As we shall see again later, the notion that Christian faith arises out of the failure of timid people to face and come to terms with the hard facts of life becomes ludicrous when we consider what manner of man Jesus was. He Himself provides the greatest example of what Bonhoeffer insisted upon in his last letters, that God speaks to men in their strength and not only in their weakness, and that the gift He grants is that of maturity, the fulfilment of true manhood. Jesus would have been con-scious not only of His own personal potentialities but also of those of mankind, for He thought of Himself not as an isolated individual but as a representative man. When, therefore, He contemplated all the kingdoms of the world and the glory of them, He would have thought of the wonderful richness and variety of life on this earth and all the power and creative ability which had been placed in the hands of mankind. Why, then, need He trouble about God? Do not the Scriptures say that no man has seen God at any time? Is it possible that the reason for this is that God is not there to be seen? Cannot the whole religious history of Israel be understood as the story of a people who defined themselves in relation to an idea of a mysterious Other called God, whose existence fulfilled a real psychological need at certain crucial stages in their development but which had performed its function so admirably that it was now no longer required? Israel had come of age. Jesus was the fulfilment of Israel, the geatest of her sons. Why not set Himself up as the founder of the new Israel, the crown and climax of self-redeemed humanity?

Let it be noted again that this is not a temptation of the naïve and irreligious. On the contrary, it is the last bastion of the religious defence against faith. This is the final and decisive test, and when Jesus has passed through it, He is ready to start on His ministry. It is when men have reached a high level of spiritual achievement, often through their own faith and that of their fathers, and have, as a result, become rightly confident of their ability to handle their own lives and master the world about them, that they become most ready to say that they have no need of a God outside themselves. It is of great significence in this context that the New Testament, and especially the Gospels, should be so preoccupied with the perils of riches. This was because Israel was rich in those ways which matter most, and Jesus was the richest of all her sons. The reason why Jesus, 'looking upon the rich young ruler loved him', may have been that He saw in the young man a reminder of his own confrontation with the third temptation. The rich man finds it hard to enter God's kingdom because he knows that riches are good and give him dominion over the kingdoms of this world and tempt him to say 'My power and the might of mine hand hath gotten me this wealth'.[1] This is why there is so much overt and covert humanism in our own time and why, to the extent that we and our children succeed in building up a prosperous and peaceful world, we are likely to hear more of it.

Jesus confronted this temptation squarely, in its full magnitude, in His own experience. We are told that He was taken up into 'an exceeding high mountain' and that he apprehended the glory as well as the extent of all the kingdoms of the world. We can be sure, therefore, that when He replied to it with the words of the First Commandment, we must not take this to be simply the conventional invocation of an authoritative word of Scripture in order to silence the equally conventional figure of Satan. Satan is routed by the decisive truth contained in the

[1] Deut. viii. 17.

First Commandment. Jesus repels him by recalling how that
Commandment arose at the beginning. It arose out of the twofold fact which we have already spoken of, that the God of
Abraham, Isaac and Jacob met them as One who was other and
greater than they were and that He was also their Saviour.
This God was a jealous God, not because He was arbitrary
and capricious, but because His reality was final and excluded
all other possibilities of final reality. Once men had met
this God, they could not worship any other God, least of all
themselves. And this God was also the One who had delivered
Israel from the house of bondage when Israel was unable to
deliver herself. Man has great possibilities in this life, the kingdoms of this world and the glory of them can be given into his
hand, but only if he recognizes that he receives them first from
the hand of God, to whom alone belongs the sceptre and the
crown. We owe our power to His grace, who has made us His
children and the heirs of His kingdom. And we cannot exercise
that power unless we first recognize our own weakness and need
without God and the necessity to seek first His kingdom and
His righteousness. It is this which Jesus sees and it is this which
enables Him to repel the attack of unbelief by reaffirming the
First Commandment.

I believe also, although it has to be admitted that no com-
mentator known to me has suggested this, that the long account
of the passionate debate between Jesus and the Jews, which takes
up so much of the middle section of the Fourth Gospel, can be
appropriately read as in some ways an externalization of the
conflict expressed in the Temptation story in Matthew. This is
particularly true of Chapter 8. The struggle which, in the
Temptation story, takes place within Jesus' mind now becomes
one between the Jews as spokesmen of the empirical Israel and
Jesus as the servant of the Lord. The Jews, like Satan, constantly
quote Scripture against Jesus and imply that, if Jesus were truly
come from God, He would do the things which Satan tries to
persuade Him to do. This is why He boldly asserts that the
Father of the Jews is the Devil.[1] Whatever the historical basis of

---

[1] See John viii. 44.

the actual statement, it would have been an intolerable act of presumption to have said it, even on Jesus' part, if He had not been tempted to take the same road as they had and had been led to see how evil it was. The devil in the Fourth Gospel is the one in whom there is no truth, who does not dwell in the real world, who is the father of lies, the source of all denial of reality. This insight, however, is itself possible only because the reality of God has been confirmed in Jesus' experience by proving itself stronger than the devil. Jesus can only say these things because doubt has been faced and overcome, because not only his own faith in God but the devil also has been tempted, tried and found wanting. Truth in the Fourth Gospel means much more than accurate statement. It is that in which we are able to live and which sustains us in freedom because it has reality. It shows us our proper natures and how to act in accordance with them.[1] This is why Jesus is able to go on to say, 'In very truth I tell you, if anyone obeys my teaching he shall never know what it is to die.'[2] Death is the most striking manifestation of non-being, of the lie which contradicts the fact of God's good creation and which is the devil's most powerful work. But the man who knows the truth is free from the threat of passing away into nothingness. Nothingness, as Barth has made us see so vividly, has no place in his abounding life. It is cancelled out and its pretension of reality is exposed.[3] The discovery that God is real and that He is stronger than all the forces which deny His reality and that He himself shares in the eternal life of God[4] is what enables Jesus to press forward with His ministry, despite the hostility of those who claim to serve God but who do not, in fact, worship Him in the same spirit as was in Jesus and in the real world where God, the source of reality, dwells.[5]

It is when we come to the story of His Passion that the nature

[1] See C. H. Dodd, *The Interpretation of the Fourth Gospel*, pp. 170–9 (Cambridge, 1953).

[2] John viii. 51 (N.E.B.).

[3] See K. Barth, *Church Dogmatics*, 3, 3, pp. 349–69.

[4] 'Before Abraham was, I am', John viii. 58.

[5] John iv. 24.

of the issue between faith and unbelief as it presented itself to Jesus stands most clearly revealed. As far as we can see, the issue in the Agony in the Garden is not so much, as it was in the Temptation, one of casting doubt on God's purpose as it was one of doing so in the most concrete way, upon His reality. The Agony and the prayer that, if it be God's will, this cup should pass from Him are occasioned not by any questioning on His part of God's power nor by any natural human desire to shrink from the ordeal of the Cross which lies before Him but by His reluctance to accept the grim fact that mankind can only be saved in the hardest way, by having it demonstrated to it that the judgment on sin is nothing less than death. It is caused by His grief that, coming to His own, 'His own received Him not.' He has to bear the burden of the knowledge that all that sinful men, for whom He could have done so much that was positive and joyful, are prepared to allow Him to do for them is to die on their behalf and in their place, so that they can know the power of His risen life henceforward only in the fellowship of His sufferings. Yet to face the fact of sin is always to be confronted with the threat of unbelief, and here Jesus faces the fact of sin in its starkest and most direct form.

It is for this reason that it is in His passion and death that the faith of Jesus in God's purpose and reality received its ultimate test. He retained His humanity to the end. This is what makes the affirmation put into the mouth of Jesus in the high-priestly prayer in the Fourth Gospel so significant of His attitude as He approached the Cross. 'Sanctify them in the truth; thy word is truth. As thou didst send them into the world, even so sent I them into the world, and for their sakes I sanctify myself, that they also may be sanctified in truth.'[1] On a more fundamental level and in a more radical way than could ever be possible through intellectual formulation and discussion alone, the issue is decisively joined concerning the reality or otherwise of God and it is in faith in God's reality and on behalf of His brethren that Jesus goes into the fight. Christian preaching and devotion have always seen this to be true in relation to sin thought of

[1] John xvii. 18–19.

primarily in terms of moral disobedience and defiance of God, but it has not emphasized sufficiently that moral evil is only one aspect of what denial of God means. When the crowd abused Jesus and cried, 'If thou be the Son of God, come down from the Cross,' and when the chief priests and scribes and elders mocked him, saying, 'He saved others; himself he cannot save. If he be the King of Israel, let him now come down from the Cross, and we will believe him. He trusted in God; let him deliver him now, if he will have him,'[1] when they said these things, this was a more direct and deadly challenge than any formal denial could be. They were saying that Jesus' interpretation of the will of God was wrong. Since Jesus had demonstrated conclusively in His ministry that He was being faithful to the essential spirit of the Old Testament, this amounted to saying that the God of Abraham, Isaac and Jacob, Moses and the prophets, the God of Israel, did not exist.

But the challenge is carried further even than this. In both Matthew and Mark, so far are these taunts from being answered that we are told that as Jesus remained hanging on the Cross and the life drained away from Him, He cried, 'My God, my God, why hast thou forsaken me?' Two considerations must always be held firmly together when, in penitence and humility, the Church meditates upon this awful cry. The first is that it must be taken as a cry of genuine dereliction. It is true that these are the opening words of the twenty-second psalm, which finishes as a triumphant affirmation of faith in the living God. But this shows only that Jesus was identifying Himself fully with God's faithful servant Israel, who endures the hiding of God's face from him and the apparent impotence of God to help him in his extremity. It in no way minimizes the reality of the experience of dereliction. The apostle says that He who knew no sin became sin for us. Sin means turning one's back upon God, the source of all life, and, since God is God, the judgment on sin is death. In His identification with mankind in its estrangement from God, Jesus endured what the rest of us, with our limited imagination and fundamental lack of seriousness, are unable

[1] Matt. xxvii. 40–3.

fully to apprehend or to sustain, the withdrawal of the preserving grace of God. The nihilistic urge of the 'world' cut off from God found unchecked expression through Him, for He went into death not, as many men do, as an insignificant incident but with the most complete awareness of the meaning and possibilities of life. Indeed, the Church, meditating upon the meaning of His life in the light of what issued from it, went further even yet and spoke of Him as descending into Hell, carrying His identification with mankind estranged from God beyond the range of this life into the place beneath the earth where the departed spirits flit aimlessly, accepting the challenge of that which denies God at the place where it appeared to hold undisputed sway. Speaking from the point of view of ordinary human experience, Jesus gave Himself up to death and to all the denial of what He had taught about God's kingdom of truth and love, allowing it to do its worst to Him.

The second consideration which must be held in mind when we meditate upon Jesus' cry of dereliction is that we find it in the Gospel, 'the Gospel of Jesus Christ the Son of God'. It is preserved and handed down to us by the Church not as an incident in itself, nor as the end of the story, but as one moment in the revelation of the living God through Christ. Jesus entered into the darkness of death and because He dwelt in the light as no man did, the darkness was deeper for Him than for any other. Yet although God was not visible to Him, He went as God's servant and even in the darkness remained in God's kingdom. The nihil was permitted to overwhelm Him, but only in order to demonstrate that although the darkness it created could 'comprehend' man, it could not 'comprehend'[1] the light of God's eternal kingdom. This is why the Church was able to dare to put the cry of dereliction in the Gospel. This is why John, writing in the Spirit in the light of the finished work of Christ was able to see the Cross as the exaltation of Christ and to put the words 'It is finished', '*Consummatum est*', in place of the cry of dereliction. The Church knew that through the power of the risen Christ it was able to continue the psalm from which the

[1] John i. 5.

cry is taken and to sing 'All the ends of the earth shall remember and turn unto the Lord: and all the kindreds of the nations shall worship before thee. For the kingdom is the Lord's: and he is the governor among the nations.'[1]

It is here that the whole argument concerning the reality of the God revealed in Jesus Christ reaches its decisive point. Rejected by human religion and surrendering all the natural vitality and rationality on which life on this earth depends, Jesus went up to the Cross and into the darkness of death, in the belief that, when all else, even his own faith as a man, had gone, God, the Lord, would remain. It was through the discovery that God honoured this faith beyond faith of Jesus in the 'sign' of the resurrection that the Church of Jesus Christ was born.

That faith in the Christian God should turn on faith in the risen Christ has always been a stumbling-block to many people, from the earliest days onward. Yet if the 'cruciality' of the Cross is fully recognized, it is hard to see how it could possibly be otherwise. All that can be said against the reality of God is concentrated in the lifeless figure of Jesus Christ upon the Cross. If this is the end as far as He is concerned, the last word is with the Nihil. Not only does this mean that all that followed the Crucifixion, the descent of the Spirit, the founding and extension of the Church, the present influence of Christ in the Spirit, becomes a monstrous, irrational enigma—that has often enough been pointed out—but it also means that all that has gone before is drained of meaning. Jesus was mistaken and misguided and His teaching can only mislead men. To cherish the Teacher of Galilee but to refuse to recognize the risen Christ is to be merely sentimental. To believe in the God of Abraham, Isaac and Jacob and to accept that for Jesus Christ the Cross was the end is to create insoluble dilemmas for that faith.[2] Here sin and death conspire to do their worst. If there is no sign that Jesus has done anything other than go the way of all flesh, we are still left in the

---

[1] Psalm xxii. 27–8.

[2] Can one any longer really be a Jew, can one endure to read the Old Testament, without in some sense, however brokenly and indirectly, believing that God raised up Christ and vindicated His faith?

presence of sin and death and are able to do nothing except submit to their power.

Experience shows, however, that those who have been driven to insist on the truth of this and to believe that it is impossible to state the main issue too sharply, must be particularly careful not to obscure this main issue by giving unnecessary attention to secondary matters or by trying to ask people to believe what they cannot and were never intended to believe. Faith in the risen Christ means faith in His present reality and power in the Spirit, a faith which was evoked in the first disciples by the 'sign' of the resurrection appearances. At this time of day, we cannot come to belief in the risen Christ through conviction of the historicity of the empty tomb and the resurrection appearances. The first disciples were in a unique situation. They had seen the crucifixion of Jesus, they had all forsaken Him and fled. Christ no longer had any living Body in the world. Before they could be brought to the place where they could give attention to God's ongoing purpose, they needed concrete assurance, from beyond the confines of present human experience, that Jesus' faith had been vindicated and that the power of God which was present in Him was going forward according to His purpose and that there was redemptive work for them to do. Like Moses at Horeb, they needed a sign, a mighty sign, to compel them to turn aside to see and to give heed to the Word of their Lord. The risen Christ appeared to them in the midst or in the way, therefore, and spoke His Word of forgiveness, peace and new life. But, in themselves, the resurrection appearances could be convincing only to those who experienced them. What makes them credible to us is the knowledge that has come to us, not only through the testimony of the apostles, but also in our own encounter with God in the Spirit, that the Lord is risen indeed and that we have to live out our lives in His presence.

That this is so is proved by the way in which the story of the resurrection is told in the Gospels. The remarkable thing about this is that the Gospels do not appear to be interested in trying to 'prove' in a way which would be satisfactory to modern historians or, for that matter, to any sceptical ancient, that Jesus really came out of the tomb and appeared alive to His disciples. It is Paul who speaks of 'infallible proofs' and he was not present. If they had wished to offer such evidence, they would have made available sworn affidavits from Caiaphas and Pontius Pilate that the tomb was sealed and that the guards were set and that they also had seen the risen Christ. But they were not writing to convince unbelievers nor were they trying to base the faith of their readers on the fact that the risen Christ had appeared to them. They were writing, in the context of the whole Gospel, 'from faith to faith'. That did not, of course, mean 'from credulity to credulity'. It meant that they were writing as those who knew the reality of the risen Christ to those who already knew the same reality. The latter did not need to be convinced that Christ was risen. He was present in their midst, in the Spirit. The curious, fitful, inconsequential, almost stammering accounts of the resurrection appearances which are given by the Synoptic Gospels and the even more baffling stories of the Fourth Gospel, where the external events are almost lost sight of in the profound interpretation which is given for the Christian community, these make sense if they are read in this way. The evangelists are recounting events with the substance of which their readers are already familiar because they already know the forgiveness, peace and guidance of the Lord, the Spirit, and their purpose is either to remind them of how they appeared to them to come about or to underline their significance for the Church's life.

To claim very much for any particular interpretation of what events in the physical world, or even in the world of experience which is open to psychological study, accompanied the resurrection appearances is to go beyond the purpose of those appearances themselves. We should respect the restraint, the economy, which seems to belong to the divine use of 'signs' which indicate that He is at work in revelation and recognize that it is a 'tempting' of God even here to try to make more of the signs than they are able to offer, in order to obtain external reassurance that the resurrection has really taken place. The 'signs' of the resurrection appearances, and these include the empty tomb, the apparently

God in Christ

physical manifestations and the preparation of the sacramental meals, call the attention of the apostolic community to the presence, from beyond dereliction and death, of the living reality of Christ. Their place, as signs, has been taken for us by the Gospels themselves, of which they are part, and the living testimony of the Church throughout the ages. Their purpose is to lead us through themselves to the reality which they signify. That reality is Jesus Christ, the conqueror of death, confronting us now, in personal encounter, with the grace and truth of the only-begotten of the Father.

It is because the Cross has posed the issue between God and that which denies God beyond the point of no return that the question 'What think ye of Christ?' has to be answered in terms of the resurrection faith. If God did not honour the faith of Christ upon the Cross, there is no God. If He did and if Christ is risen and exalted and if the Spirit is shed abroad in the world, 'the total fact of Christ' presents us with the one decisive testimony which this world provides to the reality of God. Christ does for men what only God can do. He overcomes the power of all that tries to contradict God and enables us to live in the peace of God and in harmony with each other as God's children. If this is an illusion, and as we shall see, while we remain in this life this possibility can never be finally banished, we are left with the question as to what can constitute reality, since in the Cross the nihil has triumphed. There is no answer to Pilate's question,[1] once he has delivered up Christ to be crucified, except from beyond the tomb. It is the miraculous, joyful discovery that an answer has been given which constitutes the Christian faith that God exists and that the light of His glory has shined upon us in the face of Jesus Christ. It is for these reasons that in the Spirit He is able to say of Himself, 'He that hath seen me hath seen the Father.' 'I am the way, the truth and the life; no man cometh unto the Father save by me.' It is because of this that the Christian community has come into existence in the world.

[1] John xviii. 38. Here also truth means reality, that in which we abide.

III

CHAPTER VI

The Qualities of Biblical Revelation

W
e have tried to make clear, in the last chapter, how the experience of Israel and its fulfilment in Jesus Christ provides us with decisive evidence concerning the existence or otherwise of God and have seen how it turns upon our interpretation of Jesus Christ's crucifixion and resurrection. What general conclusions about God's nature and His action can be drawn from the Biblical testimony?

The first is a familiar but important one. It is that this God is, in the Bible's own phrase, the living God. What the Bible confronts us with is not a series of hypotheses about the nature of the universe and its possible Author but with a series of events and an interpretation of them which have to be brought into relation with the rest of our experience. It confronts us, that is to say, with a history.

To say this is to utter a commonplace observation of modern Biblical study, but it has much more originality when it is compared with the way in which most people's minds still work with reference to the Christian faith. For when most people in Western lands ask themselves the question, 'Is the Christian faith true?' they appear to set about answering it in one of two ways. If they are people of non-reflective type, they naturally think of the kind of showing the institutions called churches are making in their own society, or of the kind of standing which they have in the circles in which they move, and they try to answer this question on the basis of whatever evidence of vitality and conviction which these institutions have to offer. Alternatively, if they are more accustomed to deal with abstract ideas, as most academically-educated people are, their procedure is to take a barometric reading of the position of a body of ideas called Christianity in the general intellectual climate of their time, and to make their evaluation of it on the basis of this reading. If its level is high, they pay it respectful attention; if it is low, they feel safe in disparaging or ignoring it. Now the state of the Christian cause or the Christian community at a particular time, especially when it is our own time, is a not unimportant part of the evidence, as we shall see in our discussion of whether Christian faith vindicates itself in history. But it is not all the evidence, nor is it the decisive part of it. The decisive question in regard to the Christian God is still asked far too infrequently. It is, what sense is to be made of the history which the Bible records if its own interpretation, that it is the history of the revealing activity of the living God, is not correct?

That this question has to be faced is obscured by the very fact that the Biblical writers are quite open in asserting that what they are presenting us with is not a so-called 'objective' account of a series of events which could equally well be presented by people who did not share their insights and their convictions. It is one which is at every point controlled by the belief of the writers that their interpretation of the meaning of the events they record is, in substance, a valid one, because it has been divinely inspired and honoured by God in the events which have followed as a result of it. The Bible is written as 'testaments', 'from faith to faith'. As we have seen, this must on no account be taken to mean 'from credulity to credulity', but rather that those who have experience of the reality of God in Christ are writing for those who have a similar experience and who will, therefore, find what they are saying intelligible. Nevertheless, this raises a complex of very difficult issues for the person trying to make up his mind about how to deal with the historicity of the Bible. Theologians have been far from unmindful of these difficulties, especially among the historically-minded English.[1] Yet it is doubtful whether, even yet, they have given them the attention which they deserve.[2] But, from the point of view of the present argument, our recognition of this difficulty does no more than drive the discussion a further step backward. Let us acknowledge that the Biblical story is told by those who are convinced of its truth and who, for the most part, are not interested primarily in trying to persuade the unconvinced of its truth. It is also told on the assumption, and this is especially evident in its most crucial sections such as the Four Gospels, that the central Reality, who gives meaning to the story, is known to those who read as well as to those who write. This is often seen as a source of great difficulty, and it undoubtedly is, but it should also be seen that, from one point of view, it makes the testimony of those who write more and not less impressive. It underlines the fact that these men, of like nature with ourselves, have been driven to believe, 'persuaded' in the strong sense in which Paul used that word, that the events, and the various interpretations of them, which they record, are explicable only on the basis of the existence of Someone not themselves, who stands over against them, who controls all things and to whom they are answerable, and who has now revealed His purpose to them.

This testimony can be ignored only if those who give it impress us as unreliable witnesses and if the nature of the testi-

---

[1] See William Temple, *Nature, Man and God*; R. H. Lightfoot, *History and Interpretation in the Gospels*; C. H. Dodd, *History and the Gospels*; and J. D. Smart, *Biblical Interpretation*.

[2] This point is made with great effectiveness, in a slightly different context, by Professor J. Langdon Gilkey in an article in *The Journal of Religion* (Chicago, July, 1961) where he says, 'What we desperately need is a theological ontology that will put intelligible and credible meanings into our analogical categories of divine deeds and of divine self-manifestation through events. . . . Without such an ontological basis, the language of biblical theology is neither univocal nor analogical but equivocal, and so it remains empty, abstract and self-contradictory.' To say that it is merely equivocal and that no effort is made in theology to provide an ontological basis is to say too much, but Professor Gilkey is undoubtedly calling attention to a real issue about which a great deal of work still remains to be done.

mony appears to be inconsistent with itself and grossly inadequate to the reality of which it is speaking. There is no evidence to suggest that this is the case. One of the arguments used by the old Protestant theologians in defence of the inspiration of Scripture was that it displayed what they held to be the characteristics of an inspired book. This is not the kind of argument which commends itself readily to our minds today but, at least, it reminds us that, on the ordinary human level, the Bible is a very remarkable collection of material, worthy of the most respectful attention of all men. Those who write it, and those whom they portray, are people of exceptional insight and power, holding their place among the greatest this world has ever seen, while the man Jesus defies all categorization. What is particularly impressive about this testimony is its unity. Once again, this cannot be conceived in quite the way in which the old theologians thought of it. There are plenty of rough edges in the Bible, as there are in life. But there is a basic community of experience, moving in and out of the mysterious darkness of life, between Abraham and Moses and the prophets and Jesus and the Apostles, which enables them to trace connections between them and to share the same universe of discourse. This stretches over the period of at least a thousand years within the confines of the Biblical record itself, let alone what comes after it.

In itself, perhaps, this community of experience stretching over a long period of time is not particularly impressive. After all, nothing is more common than for a religious tradition to be maintained unimpaired over a long period of time. Religious institutions are prone to become extremely conservative because the flame of religious vitality is not easily kindled nor readily kept burning, and people naturally concentrate on maintaining and defending what they have. Christian history itself abounds in illustrations of the fact that Christian institutions know no exemption from this temptation of the religious life. What is impressive about the Biblical history, however, is that it retains unity and its own kind of continuity in the midst of radical changes and upheavals and does so, not merely in the midst of external changes and upheavals but also through its own crises and transformations. Its unity is that of life, not that of the dead past, which can be easily arranged in patterns of meaning without any fear that fresh reality will break in to cause disarray. The people of God in Israel are a pilgrim people. Their life consists in forsaking the things which are behind and pressing forward in the belief that the Promised Land is before them. That is true in different ways both in the Old and the New Testaments. They are able to venture into the unknown because they believe that God is with them and that He is the living God, who has an ongoing purpose in which they have part. It is this which enabled Jesus, as representative of Israel, to go into the darkness of the Cross and to leave in the tomb all the traditions of the old Israel. The unity of Israel consisted, not in the traceable continuity of her history, although the eye of faith, looking back, can often find such continuity, but in the steadfast purpose of God. This is why, in the midst of all the changes of fortune and of understanding which Israel in the Old Testament experienced, and all the radical transformations which the new Israel had to undergo, breaking away from the Law, the Promised Land and the earthly descendants of Abraham, they remained upheld by the conviction that they still had dealings with the God of Abraham, Isaac and Jacob, their God and their fathers' God, who would never leave them nor forsake them.

This truth, familiar as it is to modern Biblical students, must be emphasized because it remains in sharp contradiction to what is widely believed in these days, even among some of those who profess the Christian faith. These approach the Bible as the most notable and worthwhile document in the story of the religious quest of mankind. They treat it, that is to say, in a fundamentally humanist way. They see the Bible as an account of men who, reflecting upon the meaning of life in general, are led to conclude that there must be a God behind it all. They pass on this idea to their children, who find the idea acceptable but who, more or less, progressively refine and generalize the idea, although they also try to express it in stories, legends, poems and elaborate accounts of wonderful deeds. Finally, a great teacher arises, more gifted in religion than any who have gone before, who outshines them in wisdom, aptitude of expression, and the ability to practise what he preaches. To call this the liberal picture of Jesus is to be unfair to the complexity of the liberal movement in theology and to its many positive achievements, but it is a picture which has gained wide currency in many modern Protestant churches and even more, and more seriously, in modern Protestant Sunday Schools. It is, of course, right to see the Bible as an account of the religious history of Israel but to see it only in these terms is to evade the challenge of revelation which is its distinctive characteristic. It is to refuse to pay serious attention to what the men of the Bible themselves say. However well-intentioned this approach may be, it cannot be absolved from responsibility for making Christian faith seem tame, ordinary and obvious, and therefore insignificant and irrelevant to our deepest needs. It is this, far more than any difficulties created by modern science or by the failures of churches to be fully obedient, which is the greatest difficulty in the way of effective communication of the Christian faith today.

The God of the Bible is not presented to men as a hypothesis, whose reality emerges only on the fringes of their consciousness. He comes into the midst of the human situation and confronts men in personal encounter. The continuity in the experience of Abraham, Moses, Elijah, Jeremiah, John the Baptist and Jesus in His humanity, together with all who come after who claim to know His Spirit, lay in the fact that they all believed that they were confronted by Another, who laid the constraint of His will upon them. The point about this constraint was that God's will was different from their wills, and yet they knew who it was of whom they were speaking when they spoke to each other across the generations. This will has its own logic and its own internal coherence, which they were able to recognize when they saw it and which enabled them to check what each said about it, yet it is a will which can never be simply deduced from what has gone before. God remains the Lord in His revelation and the direction of His purpose is kept firmly in His hands. He is constantly bringing out of His treasure things new and old and what they are we cannot tell in advance. The continuity, as we say, is impressive, but the remarkable thing about it is that it never becomes visible in those whose primary concern is with the maintenance of continuity. Otherwise, God would have spoken through the rulers of the Jews rather than through Jesus. The faith of one generation of believers is reaffirmed and vindicated in that of another, but this is no automatic process. It is possible only through the renewed venture of faith through personal commitment into the hands of the living God.

The fact that God's dealings with men are personal in this sense is an indication of His living reality, but this is not to say that it is merely 'subjective' in the other sense in which that word is used, having its reality only in the mind of man, with no discernible check upon the way in which it develops other than that provided by the inclination of the person having the idea or, at best, the peculiar internal logic of the idea itself. There is a sense, of course, in which it is true that all ideas are 'in the mind', and that includes the ideas we have of God, but, as Anselm saw in his own way, it is the peculiar characteristic of the Biblical idea of God that it tries in every way open to it, to indicate that it is not *only* an idea in the mind. For there is nothing upon which the Bible insists more strongly than that God's revelation cannot be manipulated by men to suit their convenience and that it receives a historical vindication. The call of Abraham did lead to the foundation of Israel and the call of Moses to the Exodus, the Law and the settlement in the Promised Land. The expectation of the prophets led to the coming of the Messiah. Above all and decisively, as we have seen, the surrender of His Spirit into His Father's hands by Jesus upon the Cross did lead to the resurrection faith of the Church and its conviction that it was led by His living Spirit. Outside the range of the Bible, the conviction of the apostolic church that the Gospel was for all men and its proclamation to the Gentiles has led to the extension of the Christian community all over the world. This has certainly not happened in such a way as to answer all questions. As we shall see, particularly in our penultimate chapter, it has posed many new and difficult questions. Yet the fact remains as a fact of history, if history presents us with historical facts at all, that as men have walked this way new and clearer paths have opened before them. This at least suggests that this is more likely to be the way that leadeth unto life than a pathway to a mirage.

It is this living, historical character of Christian revelation which marks it off from the speculative religious systems which have abounded in ancient and modern times. It is a disconcerting fact that it is easy enough to produce an elaborate system of religious ideas which can make some kind of sense in the minds of those who create them and also in the minds of those who are converted by them to the understanding of a few key ideas. The Gnostics at the time of the early Church and such bodies as the Rosicrucians or the Mormons or the Christian Scientists in modern times provide us with examples of this. But the Christian experience of God arose out of a meeting with God in historical events which throw light on past events and cast a beam into the future. All interpretations by Christians must be checked and disciplined by reference to history if they are to sustain themselves, even though it is true that at best any reference to the action of God in history may have to be 'analogical' rather than 'univocal'.

The living, historical character of revelation is a repeated source of assurance of faith to the men of the Bible. We have insisted that their way of questioning God's reality was to question His purpose. This questioning is not in the forefront of the consciousness of the apostolic church. The mighty events of the life, death and resurrection of Jesus Christ and the descent of the Spirit dominated their experience and they were living in the first excitement of their impact upon them. It was not until persecution overtook them that the question of whether God's hand could be discerned at work in history became again an urgent one for them, as it had been for their fathers in the Old Testament. This is why they have to be assured that they must not think it strange that a fiery trial should descend upon them.[1] This had been the experience of the people of God throughout their history. The prophets and the psalmist found constant

[1] I Peter iv. 12.

encouragement in the knowledge that their God had acted in history.[1] Whenever, in the press of events, they wondered whether God had forsaken Israel, they fell back upon the facts that this God had delivered their fathers from Egypt, had given them the Law and settled them in the Promised Land. These could not be controverted. If these were not facts and if the interpretation put upon them in Israel was not substantially valid, their fathers were deluded fools and the whole long, unique history of Israel was dissolved into meaninglessness. If, then, God had truly acted in the past, was He likely to desert them in their present extremity? So strong was their confidence in God's action in history that, with the bold anthropomorphism of the Old Testament, they sometimes used it as a basis from which they tried to stir Him up to more vigorous action in carrying on the work to which He had so determinedly set His hand in the past.[2] When God appeared to be indifferent, their conviction of His action in history was so firm that they did not lose faith but used this as proof, not that He had forsaken Israel but that Israel had forsaken Him[3] and needed to turn back to Him in penitence and expectancy. When this happened, God received them and blessed them and enabled them to carry on His purpose, not clearly and unambiguously but sufficiently definitely to lead to the coming of Jesus Christ and the Church.

The other conclusion we draw from the character of the Christian revelation of God is no less important. God in Christ is not only the living God who acts in history; He also acts as the One who is the source and end of creation, the Lord of all men and all things. Here again, we are confronted by the paradoxical quality of the Christian Gospel, which makes it seem to be foolishness to those who, in the traditional phrase, do not 'know the Lord Jesus Christ'. That a universal God should be held to have revealed Himself only in particular events is scandalous to the minds of some and that these particular events should have to carry the weight of a universal revelation is

[1] Psalm cvii. 43.
[2] Psalm lxxiv. 20–23.
[3] Isaiah lix. 1–2.

scandalous to others. How can a God who claims to be the King of all the earth limit at least His overt revelatory action to one series of events in the life of one group of people, and a very small, obscure and contentious group at that? Surely a God who is universal is much more likely to speak in a way which seems reasonable to Bishop Butler and other eminently sensible men, through laws which are discernible from the general character of nature, history and the human mind? We said earlier that the hand of God is discernible in these only in the light of His special revelation. Should not the truth, after all, be the other way round? Any knowledge of God which comes through the series of events recorded and interpreted in the Bible should be brought to judgment at the bar of this more general knowledge, which ought to be as much the subject-matter of theology as the Biblical story.

We may agree that, in one sense, this ought to be the situation but must go on to say that the fact that God chose this particular way of revealing Himself proves that it is not. God should be discoverable by man on his own resources, but the trouble is that man has refused to find Him. As Kierkegaard makes clear in his famous parable on the 'scandal of particularity', the King has to come incognito because the people are unable to recognize Him as their King. It may have been 'odd of God to choose the Jews' but, in the light of His having so chosen, we can see a certain appropriateness in His taking this action, in that the very obscurity of the Jews served to underline what He was trying to make mankind see, that in its pride and wilfulness it had turned its back upon its true King. Christ came not merely to reveal God but to reveal God in delivering men from their sin.

We sometimes make it unnecessarily difficult for ourselves to accept the 'scandal of particularity' by continuing to think of sin in excessively moralistic terms. This fails to do justice to the way in which sin works even in relation to the moral aspects of experience themselves, because it often assumes that sin consists in failure to conform to a known and already formulated moral law. But, as the Epistle to the Romans shows, this is not how sin works in the moral realm. The root of sin lies in man's refusal to recognize God's lordship and in his attempt to do that which is right in his own eyes. The Old Testament Law is not a codification of a law already written in men's hearts, in the sense that it is objectively visible for all to see. It is the fruit of the beginning of God's special revelatory act, setting man on the road which will enable him to discover his true nature again in communion with God. And it makes increasingly clear that conscience, so far from itself providing a guide to right conduct, is, apart from divine illumination, much more truly thought of as the place where man's estrangement from his true nature is most clearly revealed. This truth comes home with unique practical urgency in the moral dimension of experience but it holds for all other parts of man's life as well. Man is estranged from God and no longer possesses categories into which God can be made readily to fit. Being cut off from the kingdom of light and love which is his true home, he fumbles about in the dark, conscious that he has a home but unable to describe it properly or to bring himself to go to look for it with a genuinely practical and serious intent. What we have said in earlier chapters about mystery and the light shining in darkness is seen in its proper setting when it is seen in relation to the cross and the resurrection of Jesus Christ. Man cannot find God in the depths of his being because the further he looks into himself, the more acutely he becomes aware of his estrangement. It is only when God comes into the midst of men and re-establishes His kingly rule that men are again able to find Him and themselves and a right relation to each other.

The knowledge of what God has done for us in this way, and the understanding which that knowledge brings of the relation between God's kingdom and our human efforts to order our lives, is what enables us to accept the paradox of the particularity of God's revelation and not be merely bewildered by it. It is we who are in a self-contradictory position and, when God comes to us, He has to overturn our expectations of how He should act. Because of our need, He has to come right into the midst of our human situation, identifying Himself with us that He might help us where we cannot help ourselves. But because of our sinful pride, He had to come incognito, as a man like we are, unhindered by the irrelevant trappings of divinity according to human conception, so that we show our true natures as men by the way we react to Him. There must both be identification and encounter. Again, we say this not on the basis of any *a priori* idea about how God should act but in the light of our knowledge of how God has acted. And it is the conviction of those who have met God in this encounter that He meets them, in the particularity of a personal meeting, not in virtue of anything peculiar about them as individuals, but on the level of the human nature which they share with all their fellows. It is in this sense that what Tillich says about the most universal being the individual is true. It is the character of *this* individual which makes Him to be universal. The reality which meets them in this particular man at this particular time and place has significance for all men, whatever their time and place.

Whether this claim is justified is not a question which can be answered by saying that its truth can only be seen from the inside. Even 'from the inside', its truth has to be vindicated again and again in the changing circumstances of life in the face of new facts and new experiences which appear to impugn its reality. And from the outside, the very particularity of the history of revelation must make it seem to be no more than one chapter in the long story of human religion, for which its devotees are making extravagant claims. In modern times, when the horizons of human experience have been so greatly enlarged, the temptation to try to explain it away in relativistic terms is greatly intensified. As we shall try to see in the last chapter, the relativity of a great deal which men in former generations regarded as absolute must be frankly acknowledged. Yet even from the outside, the ability of the Christian Gospel to commend itself as true to men of the most widely differing race and background and psychological history and levels of education is an impressive indication that when Christians say that the universal God has met them on the level of their fundamental humanity, they are not talking nonsense.

We put this in this extremely cautious way because this is no more than an indication and not a proof. Here we are caught up very fully in the relativities of history and it would be mistaken zeal indeed for Christians to claim too much on this level. The Spirit of Christ is shed abroad among men and ranges much more freely than in the days of the flesh of Jesus Christ, but it still operates on the basis of particularity, through the specific calling of some rather than others, and not as a general principle clearly discernible to all men. And since the coming of the Spirit, we are still in the midst of ambiguities and enigmas. We have to acknowledge, for example, that it seems much more difficult for men in some cultural and religious traditions to give heed to Christian revelation than it is for others. The case of Islam is only the most striking in point. Much of the success, as well as a good deal of the failure, of modern Christian missions in Africa and the East, is obviously linked with the expansion of the power of Western, and especially English-speaking nations. Yet, equally, it has yet to be proved that there is any human situation into which the Spirit of Christ can have no entry because it is shown to be out of date and irrelevant. The continuity of experience which we have noted in the Bible is not less impressively visible in the much wider world into which the Christian community has moved since Biblical times. The incarnation of Jesus Christ represented a *kenosis*, a self-emptying, on his part of the fullness, range and power of the divine being. We are now in the period where the movement of Christ is towards *plerosis*, fulfilment, as the first chapter of Ephesians makes clear. The *plerosis* will not be made completely known to men while we remain on this earth, at least as far as any of us can see. This raises difficulties, which may from time to time become acute, for Christian understanding and, therefore, for Christian faith, which we shall be looking at in more detail in our chapter on the justification of God. But it is a genuine indication that the movement towards *plerosis* has taken place that the Gospel is proclaimed in Jerusalem and Antioch and Rome and to the uttermost parts of the earth and that Christ is able to break down the middle wall of partition between Jew and Gentile and to create a single new humanity, giving peace to those who are afar off and to those who are near.[1] Ever since the day of Pentecost, men of all races and cultures and periods of history and previous religions or lack of them, have found it possible to speak, each in his own tongue, of the wonderful works of God.

It is not the adumbration of this in external history, however, which is decisive here. It is the character of the experience itself to those who have it, although it must be insisted that it is of the nature of the experience that it is a common one to many people, which radically affects their relationship with each other. The knowledge of God through Christ in the Spirit which this experience brings is that of One who meets men not as a possible hypothesis to be considered among others but as a Being who compels an exclusive decision about ultimate Reality, since it is impossible for us to conceive of any Reality lying behind Him. This is partly because, to put it negatively, it gives the fullest value to the questions posed by human existence for men about their nature and ultimate destiny, and having done so, gives an answer which those who hear it and act upon it discover to be of enduring sufficiency. This is not to deny that there are large areas of common human experience to which the Christian Gospel, especially in the forms in which it is customarily presented, does not seem to be directly relevant. In our own time, this is particularly true of much technological activity. Yet, even here, those who know Christ will want to claim that our failures are due to our insensitivity to the wide-ranging action of the Spirit, our inability to grasp the Christian faith in a sufficiently 'ecumenical way', rather than to any deficiency in that faith itself. And the nearer we come to the ultimate levels of life, where the question concerning meaning becomes more personal and important, the more relevant the answer of Christian faith becomes. What is distinctive of this faith is that, out of a particular small part of human history, insight is given which enables men of all types to see the meaning of their own lives and to find the basis for a right attitude to their neighbours and to the natural world around them.

[1] Ephesians ii. 15, 17.

The Qualities of Biblical Revelation

As we say, it is the decisiveness, the cruciality, of the revelation of God in Jesus Christ which makes this to be so. The revelation is that of the *lordship* of God in Christ, in its very essence, a lordship demonstrated in conquest over that which denies it. There are many important and interesting questions about our ideas of God and His relation to the world of which the men of the Bible seem unaware and for which we cannot look to them for answers. One of the first principles of sound Biblical interpretation is to make sure that we are not looking to the Bible to provide us with answers to the wrong questions. But the one radical all-important question which it does raise, that concerning God's lordship and His purpose of love, it answers decisively, even if not, while sin remains as a reality in our midst, as yet conclusively. The Epistle to the Hebrews, in speaking of the sacrifice of Christ says that, in contrast to the sacrifices of the Temple in the Old Dispensation, it is once-for-all. Because it sets men right with God and establishes God's kingdom, this is true of Christ's work of revelation all along the line. If He is truly Saviour, Christ is also truly Lord. It is upon this belief that God, the final reality, is personally present in a unique way in Jesus Christ that the whole Gospel turns. Unless we are driven to this conclusion, we cannot know what to make of Jesus Christ. As the liberal theology of the last generation found, 'the riddle of the New Testament' becomes insoluble, because the mystery of human existence is not adequately apprehended. The questions with which man is confronted in the cross and the resurrection of Jesus Christ are evaded. To maintain anything less than that God is here uniquely and decisively present is to find ourselves with no answers to the very questions which He has pressed upon us with intolerable seriousness.

Simone Weil has said, 'Love and suffering create places in the heart which were not there before.' This is supremely true of Jesus Christ, who suffered and loved the most and, in the process, has created new hearts within us. Since God has taken the initiative through Him, none of us, whether we choose to call ourselves believers or not, can remain as we were before and refuse to pose the issues concerning life's meaning in His way. He exerts no pressure upon us to face those issues in ways which do violence to our personal freedom and power of initiative. If we do not like it, He invites us to go away in the same way as He invited the disciples to go away when many refused to walk with Him any more.[1] But anyone who has really listened to what He has to say and been subject to the influence of His Spirit knows that it is impossible to answer except in Peter's way: 'To whom shall we go? You have the words of eternal life.' Once our longing for true life and the depth of our estrangement from it have been so decisively exposed as they are in our meeting with Jesus Christ, we know that, if we cannot find ultimate reality in Him, ultimate reality is not to be found.

[1] John vi. 66–7.

CHAPTER VII

Is Christian Faith Self-Deception?

This question is inescapable, but the very fact that this is so means that it is not an original, or a peculiarly modern question. Faith always exists in tension with unbelief. That tension, as we have seen, is at its sharpest in the event of revelation itself. Faith must overcome that which appears to contradict it if it is to be faith at all, because 'God requires truth in the inward parts'.

It is worth noting these points again in this context because of the continuing prevalence in some circles of the notion that to call into question the truth of the Christian faith is to create a new and revolutionary situation in the history of thought. Our Christian forefathers throughout the centuries are alleged to have possessed a commodity called 'simple faith', which could only have arisen among the naïve, unreflecting and ignorant. This has now been challenged by honest and knowledgeable 'modern men'. The further implication is that this challenge has been successful, since it only needed someone to have the courage to point out the difficulties in the way of Christian belief for its illusory character to be exposed, as though no one had ever dared to tell this Emperor that he wore no clothes. That many people have held to Christian belief after the manner of 'simple faith' is obvious, as they have maintained 'simple faith' in other gods and in beliefs on other levels of experience. We have seen that the confluence of pietist forms of Christianity with the rise of the Enlightenment has made us particularly conscious of the tensions this creates in the Western world since the late eighteenth century. But this is far from saying that Christian faith arose in the first place among the simple-minded and that it can only maintain itself as long as its truth is not radically challenged. On the contrary, our contention is that the reverse is the case.

An illusion, as Freud reminds us, is not the same as an error because it derives from men's wishes. This is why it is character-istic of it that, once the process by which it has come into existence has been explained and the point at which its victims were led by their desires to distort reality has been exposed, it cannot any longer successfully maintain itself. Indeed, the only way in which the victims of an illusion can continue to cherish it once this has happened is by turning their backs more and more upon reality and moving still further into a dream world of their own until their power of recognizing reality is lost and mental breakdown takes place. That the world of religion offers plenty of illustrations of breakdown of this kind is obvious to all. That world, as we have already emphasized, is almost as large as that of mankind itself and it contains many different kinds of places. Religious mania is a recognizable form of mental disease.[1] It can find expression through Christian religious symbols as well as through others. Sometimes, because of the tension and strain created by the heightened awareness which follows religi-ous experience in the Christian community, it can use them more readily. Yet whether this proves that every kind of religious experience is illusory is a very different matter. To go on to say specifically that the faith evoked by Jesus Christ is of this character is to make a very bold claim indeed.

Perhaps some further definition of terms would be useful here. If by an illusion is meant any experience which is not directly verifiable by reference to sense-experience, measured in scientific terms, then faith in God is indeed an illusion but so is a large part, in many ways by far the most important part, of the rest of our experience of other persons. Few people, however, would

[1] See the article by Dr. Denis Martin in *Christian Essays in Psychiatry* (S.C.M. Press, London, 1957).

wish to retain this degree of logical puritanism in the use of words, since it inevitably leads us into situations where we are left with no rational guidance and where we cannot but believe that it is as possible as it is necessary to obtain guidance. A more general, but also more accurate way of approaching the matter, would be to do what we have done at the head of this chapter, and ask whether Christian faith is a form of self-deception. We might go further and say that it is a form of self-deception about man's nature and the way in which human affairs appear to order themselves, a superstition. We do not claim that this is more than a provisional definition of terms. The idea of a 'superstition', like that of self-deception, has little meaning except with reference to reality and what reality is remains a further question which cannot be disposed of with the claim that what it is is self-evident. Yet most people have a clear idea of what a superstition is and many of them take the view that Christian faith provides an outstanding example of it. It is an illusion in the dimension of mystery. We can, therefore, make progress in understanding by asking ourselves whether this view is justifiable.

Superstition is belief in a power or powers which, as the roots of the word suggest, stands above or over human life and influences it—a transcendent power or powers. It is characteristic of these powers, however, that they are arbitrary and irrational, working according to caprice, although it is alleged, not always on the basis of any obvious experience, that certain actions influence them. These actions, in turn, are arbitrary and irrational, like refusing to walk under ladders or avoiding the number thirteen. We can sum up superstition by saying that it has these three qualities in particular, triviality; arbitrariness and ineffectiveness. We can also say, as a consequence of the third of these qualities, that it is characteristic of superstition that, once we produce an adequate explanation of how it arises and how it works, it loses whatever appearance of potency it previously held. Its mystery vanishes with its power and it fades into the light of common day. Those who believe that Christian faith is self-deception may believe that it is a very sophisticated form of superstition, but superstition they must believe it to be. If so, it must display these qualities. Does it?

First, it is hard to see how it can be reasonably maintained that the Christian faith as made manifest in the Bible is marked by triviality. It treats the human situation with a sobriety, realism and seriousness such as are displayed by no other historical movement. As we shall see at a later stage in our argument, nowhere are the great issues of man's nature and destiny raised with a full awareness of their magnitude more seriously than here. If it is triviality we are looking for, we can find it in the attitude of those who have dismissed the possibility of the truth of the Christian faith but who find themselves able to 'enjoy' reading the Bible 'as literature'. This reveals a trivial attitude not only to Biblical faith but also to literature. In so far as literature is good it must be more than a pleasing collocation of sounds. It points to and illuminates our understanding of reality. If the Bible is worth reading as literature, and especially as 'great' literature, does not its subject-matter merit serious consideration in its own right? What was it which so sharpened the apprehension and developed the imagination of men that they were able to produce this literature? And what quality is it in the Bible which inspires men to produce great literature in many languages out of its translation? The answer to these questions does not prove that the Bible is a revelation of God. It does prove that the Bible is conspicuously free from the quality of triviality which is a mark of superstition.

Similarly, Christian faith is not arbitrary. The God who inspires it is holy, just and loving. It is true that the prophet exclaims that His wisdom is unsearchable and His ways past finding out, but this is not because He lacks rationality and integrity. It is only because we are so often arbitrary and find ourselves in the position where we cannot perceive the logic of His holy, just and loving will until He reveals it to us. When He reveals Himself, it is to bring order out of chaos, to name the creatures and to set them in their appointed places, to show men the right way to live and to lead them through the disorderly wilderness to their true home where they can enjoy that peace which is the tranquillity of order. Whatever difficulties God's election and God's covenant may raise, it is clear that no one who claims knowledge of them can also believe that mere arbitrariness is in control of human affairs.

Thirdly, Christian faith is effective. When Jesus comes, He speaks with authority, *exousia*, and not as the Scribes. His deed is as good as His word. When He comes, He casts out the evil spirits and exposes the futility of the idols. In its own way, the Bible had extremely clear ideas of what constituted superstition and how it differed from faith. The reason why it was driven to faith in Israel's God, the God who was in Christ, was that He was able to do what only reality could do and delivered men from the clutches of the superstitions which had previously enslaved them. All the images which the New Testament uses to try to describe the work of Christ make this clear. Men are brought from darkness to light. Whereas they were blind, now they see. Faith is a victorious struggle over the irresponsible, capricious, self-important powers which have tried to lay claim to rule over the affairs of men, of whose existence the men of the Early Church had every reason to be acutely aware. Those who know the power of Christ know His love and they discover that this love places them in a right relationship to each other and to the world. They are able to regard their sharing in this love, therefore, as the decisive proof of the effectiveness of Christ. 'We know that we have passed from death unto life, because we love the brethren.'

The effect of study and further knowledge upon Christian faith is also the reverse of that produced by superstition. The closer we get to the historical sources of that faith and the more we learn about the experience of the first believers, the more directly are we confronted by the challenge of its reality. As we have seen, the issue between faith and unbelief was raised and dealt with most resolutely of all in the experience of Jesus Himself. And the prophets and apostles who were His chief witnesses were not credulous and gullible men but those who had to be convinced against their natural inclinations, 'persuaded' in Paul's sense, of the truth of His claim. It is to the man of sceptical and self-critical temper and shrewd insight, who is prepared to thrust to the frontiers of experience, the wrestler, like Jacob, to whom the Word of God most frequently addresses itself. When it comes to this man, it comes with an overwhelming sense of its reality and fills him with the ability to apprehend meaning in the otherwise disorderly flux of existence. The reason why the Prologue to the Fourth Gospel and the first chapters of Ephesians and Colossians make such large, cosmic claims for the ascended and glorified Christ is that they had found in Him the key to man's nature and ultimate destiny. When the apostle cried, 'This is the victory which overcomes the world, even our faith', he was not making a defiant gesture in the face of an indifferent universe. It may be observed, incidentally, that even if it were no more than that it would at least be a courageous affirmation of belief in the possibility of meaning to which a humanist should respond positively from his own point of view. But what this cry really does is to celebrate the order and meaning brought into life by the power of Christ. The world, by which is here meant all created existence as it strains away from God, is driven by its perverse vitality back into meaninglessness and ultimate self-annihilation. But men find that in Christ, this destructive power is overcome. What the Early Church is celebrating in the language and against the background of the mythology of its own time is the fact of experience that in Christ men meet reality and reality which is not static and cold but living and practical. The world is now enabled to respond positively to the treatment it receives from the Spirit of Christ and to be transformed, both the interior world of personal relations and, much more brokenly and indirectly, the external world of nature.

More than this, we have said that it is characteristic of a superstition that, once its origin is explained and the way in which it exerts its influence is exposed, its illusion of reality and, with that, its power, vanishes. We find, however, that the closer we come to Christian revelation, the more the revelation itself forces self-questioning upon us and, at the same time, its mystery grows ever deeper. Yet that mystery in its turn, is of such a character that it invites us to further inquiry. Mystery and meaning grow together. This does not happen with a superstition.

Nor has an adequate explanation yet been provided of how this Christian faith comes to be. How has the Christian faith been able to work this confidence trick upon a large part of the human race, a part containing many of the ablest and most critically-minded of the race's members? It is extraordinary how little attention has been paid by unbelievers to this question. With the best will in the world, it is hard to treat the efforts of a man like Sigmund Freud, whose wisdom and insight we have so much reason to respect in other directions, to explain how this happened as anything other than derisory. If Christians are deceived, surely the way of scientific discipline demands that an effort be made commensurate with the magnitude of the issues involved to explain how, if not why, it came about that Jesus and the apostles, Moses and the prophets, were misled and enabled in their turn so powerfully to mislead others. Why cannot those from whose eyes the scales of Christian belief have dropped explain in terms which are faintly convincing, or even fresh, to those who remain blinded by that belief that they need not any longer be haunted by these mysteries but can come out into the light, grey and cold though it may be, and live like men? We cannot shut out the possibility that some day this may be done. But it is a possibility which our faith itself, rather than the performance of those who claim that that faith is self-deception, compels us to face.

To say that Christian faith meets the deepest needs of the human spirit and vindicates itself by producing the best fruit in thought and conduct is, of course, to say only what Christian apologists are constantly saying. This is the theme of a whole genre of literature, of which a book like H. H. Farmer's *Towards Belief in God* is a representative modern example, and it is the burden of innumerable sermons. Christ is the 'Answer to Human Need' and faith is the 'Secret of Victorious Living'. Karl Barth has forcibly reminded us of the dangers of using arguments of this kind to establish the truth of the Christian claim since they so easily slip into becoming ways of self-justification by the

Christian community and deflect attention from the real source of belief, which is not our conception of our needs nor our intellectual and moral achievements but the judging and reconciling action of God in Christ. The reminder continues to be necessary, yet the considerations to which this line of argument calls attention have weight when the man of faith is trying to examine the foundations of his own faith to discover whether they are illusory. The objections to 'Christian apologetics' brought by Barth become less urgent when it is seen that here, above all places, it is true that 'a man's foes shall be those of his own household' and that the person who has to be convinced above all others is not some outsider but his own self.[1] When a man does this and discovers both that it is his faith itself which prompts him to bring out into the open all objections to it and that it leads him into situations and relationships which have the stamp of reality upon them, he is compelled to believe that the objections are not valid and to find reassurance of faith.

II

This fact that faith itself provides the strongest impulse towards the self-criticism of the man of faith needs to be dwelt upon a little longer, because it is not always seen or admitted in these days and also because it is often mis-stated. The very existence of the theological enterprise as a critical discipline within the life of the Church is proof of this fact, but theology is so often thought of as an instrument of ecclesiastical self-justification that many people are prevented from seeing this. Theology falls into this trap just as much when it is trying to be 'kerygmatic' as when it is trying to be 'apologetic'. Sometimes it does so even more readily because the 'apologist' normally gives at least the impression of listening to objections which can be made to the truth of faith. Yet the Church finds it harder

---

[1] Anselm himself, in seeking understanding when faced with the threat that his faith was self-deception, had to take this road, and Barth has said that Anselm's was a classic description of the start of the theological task.

than any other institution of comparable age and importance to remain undisturbed in 'dogmatic slumbers' for very long. The voice of prophecy, and with it the voice of fresh analysis and self-criticism, can never be stilled within the Church while the Bible is kept open. Paul Tillich has observed that the Christian faith is the only major world religion which has submitted its sacred books to critical examination. It is important to see how this came about. It happened primarily not because believers felt compelled to justify the credentials of their faith at the bar of a truth derived from external sources but because they rediscovered the reality and power of the Gospel and wanted to state it in fresh ways for their own time. It is true that the 'climate of the age', which was itself partly formed by Christian influence, stimulated their minds as it did those of other men, but it is significant that Biblical criticism was, in many ways, the precursor and not the grudging successor, of the modern scientific study of documents. Biblical criticism has done much to teach historical criticism its method.

The significance of facts like this is not always clearly seen because we are unaccustomed to think of the intellectual implications of the distinctively religious notions of the judgment of God and of repentance. This is one of the regrettable consequences of the excessive moralism of post-Pietist Protestantism. Judgment, repentance and renewal of life obviously affect us most vividly and directly in the moral dimension of experience but they are not purely moral realities. Or, to put it in another and perhaps more accurate way, their moral implications are to be found on the intellectual level as well as on those of personal relationship and social behaviour. There *is* one thing which concentrates a man's mind more powerfully than the prospect of being hanged the next morning. It is a genuine experience of the judgment of the living God, piercing between the joints and the marrow, and of the renewal of life which comes from His forgiving grace, flooding the world with light and meaning.

One of the most illuminating, and entertaining, family connections observed in the recent history of thought has been that noted by Noel Annan in his biography of Leslie Stephen.

Is Christian Faith Self-Deception?

Starting from the fairly familiar fact that a large part of the intellectual aristocracy of Victorian and post-Victorian England is descended from pious Evangelical families, he goes on to show that the famous Bloomsbury set of the 1920s, the *avant-garde* of Cambridge highbrowism who have had great influence on the style of modern academic life in England, were not only the direct descendants of the members of the Clapham Sect but also displayed, in very different guise, many of the characteristic qualities of their grandparents. Similarly, it can be fairly readily demonstrated that much of the dogged intellectual vitality and the earnest self-criticism of modern American scholarship and letters is due to the fact that its exponents are often the descendants of long generations of Puritan divines, accustomed both to study and to self-examination.

Let us be quite clear about what is being implied here. I am not implying that, despite their protests to the contrary, Virginia Woolf and E. M. Forster and the rest are really Christians. What I am claiming is that they inherited and were encouraged to develop an attitude of mind which was largely produced by Christian faith. It was not the case that they were emancipated from the superstition of Christian belief through the power of an intellectual insight entirely derived from another and alien source. Faith itself, present in the community in which they were brought up, helped to produce a great deal of that power. They would not have been the kind of people they were, they would not have produced the type of criticisms of Christian belief which they did, without the formative influence of Christian belief in their background. This again does not in itself prove Christian faith to be true but it does indicate that its relation to the minds of those who have been influenced by it and who may even have gone on to reject it, is much more complex than is often supposed. It is also not the kind of relation which can be described as that produced by superstition. These people are in a very different situation from those who have emancipated themselves from a superstition. They are like members of the old Israel who enjoy the benefits of the Promised Land but find themselves unable to believe that there ever was an Exodus and who are compelled to reject the Law, which governed their upbringing and has given shape to their lives, as a tissue of deceptions. The conclusion they reach may be true, but if it is, it creates immense problems in self-understanding which, so far, even the most sensitive of the unbelieving children and grandchildren of believers seem reluctant to face.[1] The Christian believer can perhaps be pardoned for suspecting that those who find themselves in this position and yet see no critical problem for their own existence are more likely to be the victims of self-deception than he is. They remind him a little of the fifteen-year-old beatnik who said to Mort Sahl in a San Francisco coffee bar, 'The Western religions have failed me'.

The last thing we should want to claim in arguing that faith is productive of genuine intellectual vitality is that the record of religious institutions in general and Christian institutions in particular is unambiguously admirable in these respects. The enemies of religion have always been able to point to evils perpetrated in its name, and there are still plenty of them to be found. The idea that religion as such is a 'good thing' is a typically superficial modern notion which can only be held by those who patronize religion without taking it seriously. It is true that there are very few forms of religion which degrade men, although there are some, but there are plenty which shut men's eyes to important aspects of the real world and lead them to unconscious cruelty or to narrow-mindedness. Religious movements are particularly prone to the vices of excessive conservatism, partly because they feel that they must at all costs maintain their precious religious heritage against attack. Christian religious history has plenty of dark chapters within it. Some of them are darker than other religious histories can show. Christian faith releases powers in men and arouses desires in them which might otherwise remain dormant and the power of evil becomes all the more violent and desperate the nearer it is to the reality of faith. This is one reason why it is as vitally important to insist

[1] This important aspect of the matter is, for example, not directly faced in the sympathetic biography of his godly ancestor Marianne Thornton by E. M. Forster (Edward Arnold, London, 1956).

on the distinction between Christ and His Church as it is to emphasize the inseparable connection between them.

No Christian interest is served by minimizing the amount of truth that there is in all this, yet it does not alter the fact that its sternest and most discerning critics are to be found within the Christian community, and that it is the Church's Lord and not any outside interest which inspires their criticism. We might even agree that it would be a good thing if religion could be abolished from the world, but yet have to admit that the only person who can do that for us is not the scientist nor the psychiatrist nor the 'rational thinker' nor the beneficent social planner, but only God Himself, who has shown us the way in which we can transcend religion by faith working through love. Critics of the churches are apt to assume that churches claim to be perfect societies and therefore to judge them by the standard of perfection. They clearly fall far short. But if churches are regarded as what they are, communities of frail, mortal men, open to the same temptations and subject to most of the same pressures as other men, their achievements are seen in a different light. The undue conservatism of churches, for example, looks different when this is done. Christian churches, along with Jewish synagogues, are generally the oldest and most firmly-rooted institutions which still flourish in the modern world, far older than the nation-states. People always tend to be most conservative, also, about those things which are impalpable and yet affect them deeply. That there should be a great deal of conservatism in churches is, therefore, hardly surprising. What is surprising, from the ordinary human point of view, is that there should be so much self-criticism in churches, so much readiness to adjust cherished preconceptions to new modes of thought and so much courage in venturing into new situations. This gives absolutely no grounds for complacency to Christians themselves, looking at their lives in the light of God's purpose for His pilgrim people. On the contrary, in this respect more than in any others, the prophetic power of faith will exercise itself chiefly in denouncing the failures of the Christian community. Yet those who denounce the conservatism of churches most loudly will be those who see most clearly that these failures can be redeemed, not by retreat from the benighted superstition of faith into some allegedly 'progressive' humanism but by greater faithfulness to the living God in Christ Himself.

The more familiar argument in confirmation of the truth of Christian faith, that which points to its moral results, is one which the sensitive put forward with hesitation and reserve in these days. In the past, it has been grievously overworked and it is hard to put it forward without a measure of the self-righteousness which completely destroys its efficacy. Today, there are far too many reasons to be aware of the failings of so-called 'Christian civilization' for anyone to be able to use this line of argument with any self-confidence in addressing those whom our forefathers did not scruple to describe as the 'heathen'. Yet if the argument has to be severely qualified in speaking today out of the context of a very imperfectly Christianized society to those of other faiths, it retains much of its validity when Christians themselves consider whether their faith is firmly based. And it is still a justifiable *argumentum ad hominem* against those in our own society who, themselves the products of Christian nurture, lightly and arrogantly dismiss Christian faith as outworn superstition. So remote from moral realities does this dismissal often become that it begins to have a comic flavour. For it not infrequently happens that those who most frequently, and eloquently, take this line are those precariously 'emancipated', self-consciously 'intellectual' people who are notable chiefly for their stupid drinking habits, their neglect of their public duties and the messy selfishness of their personal lives. Yet, speaking very figuratively, they thank God that they are not as their ignorant, clean-living, God-fearing parents who pinched and scraped, under the influence of the despised superstition, to give their child the benefits of education, because they believed it would bring him nearer the truth and enrich all their lives. In such a situation, which is common enough in the modern Western world, it is permissible to inquire who it is who is being self-deceived. The community of believers may often be unimpressive enough. Is the community of conscious unbelievers any more impressive? May there, indeed, still be enough difference between the two, even in our mixed-up modern world, to be at least a small sign which points to the possibility that the one group has access to a reality on which the other has turned its back?

The history of the Christian community has its dark chapters. Even the best of religion can turn sour when it is not transcended by faith working through love. Its presence also stirs people up and makes evil more terrible than it was before. But the New Testament has never said that things would be otherwise. It was not merely religious men, but men brought up to know and serve the one true God, who conspired to crucify the Lord of Glory. And the New Testament decisively rules out the possibility that faith is a form of self-deception by driving men to see what no other faith does and what, of themselves, no men will admit, that even their good is not fully good and that even their truth is not without its elements of lying error. Their very highest religious achievements can themselves become the most deadly of snares unless they are humbly submitted to the judgment of God. These include, let it be said again, those which bear a Christian name and those which, in themselves, are the fruit of what was, in the first instance, authentic faith in Christ. The New Testament insists, and insists again, that at no point can any man rest assured and content with his religious status. Once he does, he is immediately in the grip of self-deception. The very fact that faith makes men see that there is far more self-deception in religion than they ever supposed, and that it can take subtler and more deep-rooted forms than any psychologist not well-versed in theology could ever uncover, is itself the surest indication that faith itself is not self-deception. It is hard to see how we can drive farther back in self-analysis than faith compels us to go or what nook or cranny of our egotism can be left unexplored after it has done its judging and purifying work.

Christians seeking understanding of their own faith must, in all honesty, put this much more strongly and positively. So far from being the product of a superstitious illusion, the characteristic of Christian faith to those who have it is that, as we have seen again and again, it is an awakening to reality, which is a gift of grace. This familiar phrase, 'a gift of grace', means precisely that it is not of our devising but granted to us by the goodness of another. And it vindicates its truth not only by the flood of healing, fulfilment and renewal which it releases in men's hearts but by the way in which it organizes their personalities and enables them to find a relationship with each other in which they bring out the best in each other. Christians, if they are speaking their minds, have to say that if this is illusion, then there can be no reality, because this is the nearest thing to reality which it has been given to man to know. To put this Christian conviction in Christian language, in Jesus Christ we recover our proper manhood, our maturity, our real natures.

If it be objected that this may prove that Christian faith meets a deep need of human nature and does so in a singularly beneficent way but does not prove that all this is caused by the action of a living, personal God, we may agree. But we were not setting out to prove the latter at this point of the argument, and the fact that Christian faith meets this need in this way is one of great significance. If the fruit of what Christians call 'knowledge of God' is the reverse of what is produced by superstition, this is evidence that they are not self-deceived and it, at least, provides a prima facie case for the claim that they are not radically misled in accounting for the experience in the way in which they do. Decisive assurance of God's reality can only be given in the moment of divine encounter we call faith. This no man can create in another. It can be done by God alone. But the believer can confront his neighbour who lacks the assurance of faith with the claim that anything which produces the results which follow from Christian faith must be something which is very much in the order of reality.

It is, perhaps, this insight which lies behind Pascal's famous 'wager' argument. As a fully-fledged argument for belief in God, as an apologetic weapon in the traditional sense, it is not likely to carry much conviction but it was hardly intended to be that by its author. It is a mathematician's fancy, which is worth pursuing because it does light up one aspect of man's experience as he thinks about the reality of God. Pascal begins by saying that he is speaking according to natural lights for the moment. That is not a phrase which will readily commend him to those who have been made conscious by Barth of the dubious status of all speaking according to 'natural lights', but that need not worry us unduly on the level of this fancy. He does not mean much more than that he is speaking superficially. He assumes, for the purposes of his argument, that, according to reason, there is nothing to choose between believing and not believing in God. This is agnosticism in its purest form. As far as a wager is concerned, heads and tails have it equally. The course which reason dictates in such a situation is that we should refuse to wager. But he asserts that it is a condition of human existence that this is a wager we have to make. If then, reason cannot help us, does happiness offer us a criterion by reference to which we might be able to make up our minds? This is more useful. If you wager that God is, you gain all. If you wager that He is not, you are in no worse case than when you started out. Realize further that, in this particular wager, there is no point in wagering anything except all you have and then decide to place it all upon your belief that God exists. What harm, he asks, befalls the one who wagers that God exists? 'You will be faithful, honest, humble, grateful, generous, a sincere friend, truthful. Certainly, you will not have those poisonous pleasures, glory and luxury; but will you not have others? I will tell you that you will thereby gain in this life, and that at each step you take on this road, you will see so great certainty of gain, so much nothingness in what you risk, that you will recognize that you have wagered, for something certain and infinite, that for which you have given nothing.[1]'

What Pascal is saying here is not so much that, in the popular phrase of so many sermons, it is worth betting your life that there is a God, with the implication that this is the least uncertain and most hopeful of a variety of prospects that life offers, rather as though this were a horse race in which one picks one's

[1] *Pensées*, 233, pp. 66–8 (Everyman Edition, Dent, London).

favourite. What he is really trying to say in his figure of the wager is that to believe in God is not really to gamble at all. He uses the figure of the wager only in order to show how inappropriate it is to the decision of faith. For all practical purposes, you have placed your money on a certainty. The alternative to the Christian way is not another and better way of life; it is misery and despair and ultimate meaninglessness. The alternatives before men are those with which the Deuteronomist confronted the old Israel, life and death, good and evil. What man in his senses, Pascal asks in effect, would choose death and evil? What, therefore, have you got to lose by choosing life? This may or may not be a convincing line of argument in itself, but our point here is that it is not a line which could be pursued at all unless the fruit of Christian faith has been the reverse of that which is the product of an illusion.

III

At this point, the objector may decide to try a different line and suggest that Christian faith may be a form of self-deception of a more qualified and subtle kind. He may agree that this form of religion at its best, like some others but unlike many more, has often performed a beneficent function in helping people to reach maturity. It is an illusion, but, let it be admitted, a helpful illusion. People need a measure of reassurance that a hostile universe will not overwhelm them and also some optimism and courage in withstanding the shocks of harsh reality. This was particularly true in the childhood of the race. It may still be true for some of us in our childish moods and for our children at the early stages of their development. Liberal Sunday Schools where young children learn about a 'father-God' do not do anybody any harm and often seem to help children through a difficult phase in their development. But as the history of many of those who pass through those Sunday Schools proves, as they grow older, people are able to put away childish things, and one of the things they naturally put away is this 'father-God'. As we grow older and more experienced, he becomes increasingly unnecessary. We become able to look reality straight in the face, to accept the limitations of human life and to use the methods of scientific investigation and technological application to achieve whatever measure of control of our natures and our environment it is possible for men to achieve. What is possible may not be all we would like but we make progress, and it is real progress. It is far better to concentrate on trying to do this rather than to go on being troubled with a 'cosmic anxiety' which will lead us nowhere and with a set of ideas which are relevant and useful only in the childhood of the race or of the individual.

Those who hold this view would argue that it is backed by solid experience. Progress towards a fuller, richer and happier life is not reached by following religious practices, but by emancipation from them or, at least, by rendering them insignificant and trivial. If we are to choose life, let us follow man and scientific technique, not the God-image of the ancient Hebrews. The way to life is the way of secularization. Where religion still holds sway in the modern world, as in India or in the Moslem lands or in large parts of the Orthodox East or in the less prosperous Latin countries, men remain in a primitive or, at least, a very backward state. It is only since they pushed religion out of the way that Russia and China have begun to make real progress. It is true that religious institutions still flourish in some, although not all, progressive Western lands. But they flourish most in those which are youngest and when they do, it is not as the truly regulative power in men's lives but as innocuous, vague and non-superstitious activities, which do as little harm as good. It is significant, too, that the most prosperous and widely popular parts of the life of these religious institutions are the Church schools for younger children and the social groups for older women. For the most part, churches are merely tolerated out of a decent respect for the past and because they have a certain modestly useful role as instruments for maintaining social cohesion in some communities. Modern men at their most characteristic, busy about their affairs in the life of the world, have little time for it, and the reason why they have little time is that they have little need. It is these modern men who are the nearest to that 'proper man' of whom we were speaking earlier, not that fading ideal figure, the Christian man. Salvation is no longer a term which conveys much meaning to modern men because they have found as much salvation as they are likely to get and have learned how to make do with it as best they can. They may not be entirely the masters of their fate and the captains of their soul but they themselves are likely to be the nearest to a master and captain their fate and their soul can find. Let religion get out of the way and allow Science in the broadest sense to carry on with the job.

It is this faith which is, and is likely to be, the most widespread and effective modern alternative faith to the Christian in our own time. It was the working faith of the Enlightenment in the eighteenth and early nineteenth centuries and it reached ever-widening circles of the educated in the Victorian and post-Victorian ages. It has now become successfully popularized, not merely through the formal presentation of its ideas but also by the emergence of a style of life, that based on the reduction of the issues of human living, including many issues of personal relations, to 'problems' which can be solved by the application of technical know-how derived from scientific discoveries, which has brought great benefits to large numbers of people. It has, in fact, now become the conventional faith of many people in the Western world, including some who find their way into churches from time to time, a faith which requires far less effort and mental adjustment to adhere to than the classic faith of Christendom. If material prosperity continues to grow and if its benefits can be extended to depressed peoples who at present do not enjoy them, it is likely to become the conventional faith of more and more people throughout the whole world.

What are we to say to this? The first thing to be said, and it cannot be said too strongly, is that the reaction to all this of those who profess Christian faith should not be purely negative.

Is Christian Faith Self-Deception?

On the contrary, the Christian will agree with a very large amount of the criticism of religion, including Christian religion, made by those who take this view. He also will insist upon the relative maturity of modern man and agree that, speaking from the ordinary human point of view, it is in man himself and not in any external influences or powers, gods or demons, that his salvation is to be found. He will agree also on the vast importance of the extension of the scientific method, whose most enlightened exponents insist that it should find a place for imaginative intuition if it is to function properly, into every area of life where it applies. Nor should he deny that we cannot say confidently in advance that there are certain areas of life from which it must be shut out. He will even agree that it represents an advance when many matters which were previously thought to be reserved for the realm of mystery are seen to be perfectly capable of handling as problems, which can be solved and cleared out of the way. This is true, for example, of many forms of mental illness or even of at least some aspects of human relationships. Job analysis and time and motion study can sometimes deal neatly and quickly with difficulties which have often taken up a great deal of time in efforts to achieve 'better human understanding', sometimes through very elaborate prayer, fasting and feasting. Christians who are distressed and disappointed by the superficiality and inadequacy of Freud's treatment of faith in *The Future of an Illusion* should not allow that fact to obscure for them the warmth and conviction with which he writes about the scientific method, used with imagination and faith, even in dealing with important aspects of human personality. This is good and, to the extent that the method is used in a truly scientific way, the man of faith can rejoice at the healing, simplifying and enriching power which it brings. He will have no fear that this will diminish the area over which the mystery of revelation operates, for the more we are able to handle life as a series of 'problems' which are capable of solution, the easier it becomes to know the true mystery of the love and power of God. As Bonhoeffer, using different terminology, has pointed out, it is a mistake to think of God as the explanation of what is left over when we have come to the end of our problem-solving capacity.[1]

In so far, therefore, as modern man is able to exercise the maturity of freedom and the ability to control his life so as to make himself and his neighbour happy and comfortable, the Christian will be glad. What he will be sceptical about are these two things. The first is the claim that he has done this on his own resources. To discover and apply the scientific method is good, but what evidence is there for the idea that the reverence before the facts, the self-sacrifice, the patience and the flash of insight into causal connections which helped to create the scientific revolution arose simply because of man's own insight and power? Does not experience constantly show that when people begin to think like that and to cry, 'By my own might and the strength of mine arm have I gotten this wealth', it happens that their insight and power over themselves and ultimately over nature also, are poisoned at the springs? Man has to get himself out of the way before he can reach the singleness of eye which is the mark of maturity and the secret of his ability to master his own soul and to determine his own destiny. As soon as he tries to be self-sufficient, he becomes proud and his vision is distorted. 'It is the Solver that is the ultimate Problem.'[2]

The most ambiguous achievement of modern science has been the discovery of the ability to make a nuclear reaction, where a secret was wrenched violently from nature in a situation where little attention could be paid to the wider consequences for life on this planet of this sudden access of new power. It may have been necessary to do it in this way, yet it is significant of the corrupting power of humanist pride that no recognition is made of this in the complacent plaque which commemorates this event on the site where it first took place at the University of Chicago.[3] It is becoming increasingly clear to all of us,

[1] See *Letters and Papers from Prison* (S.C.M. Press, London).
[2] See *Tragedy, Myth and Mystery* by Richard Y. Hathorn (Indiana University Press), p. 16.
[3] 'On 2nd December 1942 man achieved here the first self-sustaining chain reaction and thereby initiated the controlled release of nuclear energy.'

scientists and non-scientists alike, that unless we learn humility and mutual forbearance with one another in handling this power, we shall destroy ourselves and our children. And in this, nuclear power is only the most striking and violent example of all the powers which have been placed in our hands in the modern world. In the past, the place where, above all others, men have found this humility and mutual forbearance is at the foot of the Cross. What is the evidence that 'emancipated modern man' either no longer needs these or is able to find them quite adequately in other ways?

The other thing about which we are sceptical is the claim that the 'emancipation' of which we speak is in itself satisfactory or likely to be permanent. Is the modern world a place of ever-growing sweetness and light? Is its 'progress' automatic or is it any more than an enlargement of the sphere in which the ancient conflict between good and evil has to be fought out, with partial victories on some levels clearing the ground for the emergence of fresh enemies on others? Is man any less a 'problem' to himself in the twentieth century than in the nineteenth or the seventeenth or the twelfth? As we have indicated, it is unbecoming for Christian apologists to derive self-satisfaction from the decline of the evolutionary optimism of some Victorian thinkers. We can only wish that some of their hopeful prophecies had come true! The world would indeed be a happier place than it has been in our time. But we cannot shut our eyes to the fact that their prophecies have not come true nor to the other fact that as many people seek the so-called 'comfort' of one sort or another of religion today as have done so in the past. And many more people are looking for other sorts of 'comfort' of a less innocuous character, the political ideologies of our century or the retreat into irresponsible private life where they settle more or less contentedly for being a good deal less than mature human beings who are the masters of their fate and the captains of their soul.

Indeed, from some points of view, I might be prepared to agree with those who argue that since religion is a barrier to maturity it would be a good thing if religion were abolished, and with religion all the 'principalities and powers' which becloud the vision and distract the attention of men from doing justly and loving mercy and walking humbly and joyfully, at least with one another. But how can this be done? The state of the modern world suggests, as clearly as does the rest of history, that this cannot be done simply by pointing out how good a thing it would be to do. Only a stronger power than religion and the principalities and powers can cast them out. The Christian claim is that God in His self-revelation through Jesus Christ has done that. As Karl Barth says, it is faith alone which can achieve the abolition of religion.[1] That abolition will never be possible in this life, but at least faith can put religion in its proper place, and with religion, all the loyalties to the principles of reason or to nation or class or institution or family which, left to themselves, swell into 'principalities and powers' which dominate and enslave the spirit of man. Where is the 'proper man', the 'mature man', who is so desirable, to be found? The best that non-Christian faith can seem to offer is the grey and pallid creature, alone with his 'normality', whom Freud leaves us with after his spiritual bone-setting operations are completed, or the leuchotomized and harmless dullard who emerges from 'existential despair'. Where else can such a man find his humanity again, his richness and vitality and his joy, except in and through Jesus Christ? Bonhoeffer is right in his insistence that what we need to see today more than ever before is that to be a man faithful to Jesus Christ is, above all, to be a *man*, one who lives with the joy and freedom which belong to his proper nature. The goodness of the Gospel is that it is possible to become such a man by conformity to Jesus Christ. It is no clearer today than it has ever been in the past, in fact it is less, that this manhood can be found anywhere else than here.

The more the Christian believer considers what it is that has come to him in faith and how it is related to the rest of his experience, the more convinced he becomes that this is not self-deception but the means by which he finds entry into the real world. No alternative explanation seems possible which begins

[1] *Church Dogmatics*, Vol. I, Part II, pp. 280–361 (English translation).

to do justice to what he finds. This is not to say, however, that he can now take his rest. He may be convinced that in Christ he meets reality. But how securely based is this reality, and does it fulfil all the claims which it makes for itself? These are questions to which we must devote our attention in the remaining sections of our discussion.

CHAPTER VIII

Christian Faith and Human Tragedy

O ne of the characteristics of thought in the twentieth century has been the renewed emphasis, as compared with the nineteenth century, on the tragic element in human experience. We use the phrase 'the tragic element' deliberately because it has a wider connotation than the literary one alone, although it obviously must be related to it. The American literary critic, Richard Hathorn, has defined a tragedy as a 'work of literature which has as its chief emphasis the revelation of mystery.'[1] I wonder whether this is not too broad a definition, even though he allows that a tragedy, in the Christian understanding, might possibly have an ending which is, in some ways, a happy one. If this is so, it is hard to see how he distinguishes tragedy from comedy since, as we have insisted all along, mystery remains even when all is fulfilment and peace. Indeed, it is hard to see how, in a Christian as distinct from a Greek context—although it is not always easy even there—a completely consistent line can be drawn between tragedy and comedy on the level of works of the imagination. Just as 'the worst is not so long as we can say, "This is the worst", so no work of literature can ever be completely tragic. Nevertheless, there is a 'tragic sense of life', to use the title of the translation of one of the first works of the twentieth century

[1] *Tragedy, Myth and Mystery*, p. 223.

which began again to make this emphasis,[1] and it is this which has come into the forefront of the consciousness of many people in our own time.

This 'sense' has, in our view, two elements. One of them is an awareness of the rich possibilities which life holds. The other is the fear that, in the nature of the case, these possibilities cannot be fulfilled. The 'tragic sense of life' arises out of the conviction that we are creatures destined to find meaning and who yet fear that meaning may not be there to be found, that we are the victims of a cosmic trick, led on to commit ourselves to living fully and richly and then finding it all dissolve to nothingness in our grasp. It is this anxiety which is the theme of a great deal of modern existentialist writing, notably in Heidegger and Sartre, and it has found echoes in the experience of many people in many lands. One of the reasons for the power which ideologies have had over men's minds in our century has been that they have sought refuge in them from the intolerable pressures created by 'the tragic sense of life' in an age when they were unable to find their way to the sustaining of those pressures through the Christian knowledge of God. Fascism and Communism, the latter at least for members of the Western *bourgeoisie*—for someone arising out of a different milieu it could be different—are best understood as such refuges. If life has no real meaning, it is better to snatch in frenzy at anything which appears to impose a measure of meaning upon it, without being too scrupulous about examining its credentials, grateful for its apparent assurance and vitality.

This tragic sense of life, however, is evoked by factors present in the human situation as such, and is certainly not something to be completely accounted for by differences in spiritual climate between one age and another. As we saw at the outset in our discussion of the nature of the dimension of mystery, we cannot raise the great human questions without becoming aware of the intolerable contradictions of our predicament, and the more generously we give ourselves to the business of living, the more intolerable the contradictions

[1] Miguel de Unamuno, *The Tragic Sense of Life.*

become. We are creatures in whose hearts a longing for eternity has been set, and yet we have to die. The tragic element in this situation does not lie in the fact of death itself. Death can sometimes come mercifully, for man as for beast, without, in the moment of its impact, making us aware of its tragic character. The tragedy lies in the fact that we are made for life and recoil from death as the contradiction of our true nature. The more fully we give ourselves to life, the more the sting of having to die makes itself felt. Similarly, our souls respond to beauty. They long to achieve and appropriate its perfection and hold it fast for ever. Yet, in the very act of its enjoyment, beauty eludes us. Beauty heightens our sense of the significance of life without, of itself, being able to give direction to that sense, although it can point to and express that through which meaning can be found. 'The sweetest songs' are not necessarily always those which 'tell of saddest thoughts' but their very sweetness creates a sadness which, by themselves, they are unable to remove. We are aware also of an unconditional moral obligation to do the right. Yet we constantly find ourselves involved in situations where we cannot even see with any clarity what the right is, let alone find the power to do it. Above all, we long for unbroken and abiding communion with those whom we love. Yet this communion cannot be fully realized. It is this which gives a great deal of its poignancy to our frustrated longing for eternity, which would have little meaning simply as infinite duration for ourselves as individuals. But even in this life, our relationships with those whom we love most deeply are shot through with ignorance and misunderstandings. We are strangers to one another, 'problems', even while we enjoy the mystery of communion.[1] The most completely satisfactory human marriage falls short of the ideal and the sober wisdom of Christian history has always recognized that it ends with physical death.

[1] It is interesting, and significant, to note that it is this tragic element in personal relationships which Martin Buber, who has done so much to make us appreciate their primacy and richness, fails to emphasize. If he had seen it, he might have better understood the apostle Paul and the Epistle to the Romans.

Christian Faith and Human Tragedy

No interpretation of human existence can carry much conviction which does not struggle to do justice to the 'tragic sense of life'. The attitude which its exponents take towards 'tragedy' provides an even more searching test of the seriousness and realism of any philosophy than their attitude towards mystery. It is here that the unreality and the superficiality of much naturalistic philosophy is exposed and it is here, too, that the basic timidity, the academicism in a pejorative sense, of a great deal[1] of linguistic analysis is also exposed. It may indeed be true that it is better to be silent when one cannot say anything which helps, and in the case of a man of existentialist temper like Wittgenstein this may have been right, or at least an attitude which compels respect. But a great deal of linguistic analysis shrugs off 'cosmic anxiety' far too lightly, as though it were merely a matter of temperament or historical circumstance whether one knows it. The tragic hero, who launches out into the deep, realizing that life is for living, is not only more likely to discover life's meaning, he is also more fundamentally realistic than the man who engages only in careful paddling about on the beach, concerned only to avoid getting out of his depth and having to submit to the indignity of crying for help to his fellows.

The simpler kinds of idealistic philosophy, of which the Victorian world produced many examples, are open to objection from the opposite point of view. These found the answers before they had appreciated the full magnitude of the questions. They did not see the radical character of the difficulties which our failure to realize the good, the true and the beautiful present nor the ambiguity of man, the thinking subject, caught not merely between heaven and earth but between heaven and hell. One of the reasons why Christian faith seems irrelevant to the experience of many people who have been awakened to the tragic character of existence is that it has been presented to them as a form of popular idealism of this kind. This is, perhaps, particularly true of the situation in the churches of the U.S.A.

The faith of the Bible, however, is that of men who are full

[1] Again, I do not say all.

155

of the 'tragic sense of life' and who insist on facing resolutely all those facts of sin, suffering and mortality which give rise to the apprehension of tragedy. The kind of understanding of tragedy which arises among the Greeks is not to be found in the Bible. The revelatory power of God, His promise in His judgment, His loving-kindness as well as His wrath, in the Old Testament as well as the New, prevents us from having the kind of pity or terror which are to be found in much of Greek tragedy. This should make Christians read those tragedies with particular sympathy since we see these noble people, our brothers and sisters, groping in the dark. Yet, as we have seen, the threat of meaninglessness is constantly present in the Bible and an acute sense of man's frailty and weakness in the presence of powers stronger than himself. 'Man that is born of a woman is of few days, and full of trouble. He cometh forth like a flower, and is cut down: he fleeth also as a shadow, and continueth not.' (Job xiv. 1-2.) 'I have seen the travail which God hath given to the sons of men, to be exercised in it. He hath made everything beautiful in its time; also he hath set the longing for eternity in men's hearts, so that no man can find out the work that God maketh from the beginning to the end.' (Eccles. iii. 10-11.) And it is the men of faith in the Bible rather than their opponents who are constantly reminding themselves and others of the enigmatic character of life and its inexorable limits. 'Watchman, what of the night? The morning will come, the night will come also.' The ordinary so-called 'secular' man, who tries to crowd meaning into his passing experience, a meaning greater than it can bear, is the man who is indifferent to the tragic dimension, as he is to that of mystery. It is he who is intoxicated by the fact that his barns are full and who pulls them down to build greater, as though to extend his comfort and self-sufficiency beyond his mortal span. It is he who settles down to enjoy himself, forgetting that that very night his soul may be required of him.

The characteristic form of 'secularization' in the bad sense—there is a good one—is indifference to the tragic dimension of existence, indifference which is due not to having faced and overcome the tragedy nor to an insight which proves it to be illusory but to a loss of the sense of reality. Sin, Karl Barth has reminded us, expresses itself as sloth,[1] and sloth is a sign of the death of the spirit. Because Biblical revelation is an awakening to life, a fulfilment of the promises of fullness of life, it is also an awakening of the 'tragic sense of life'. The characters in a novel about members of a literary set in New York were described as 'blobs of consciousness afflicted by moral apathy'. Like the summer inhabitants of St. Tropez described by Edwin Muir whom we mentioned earlier, it is probable that their novels were not very good because 'moral apathy' is not the seed-bed of creativity. Biblical faith not only faces up in 'realistic' fashion to the grim facts of sin, evil and mortality. To do this alone confirms us in sloth and listlessness and makes us apathetic in the strict sense, unable to fight back even with the courage of existential despair. It also has the further, and greater, courage to set these squarely against our longing for holiness, perfection and eternity and to say that both must be taken fully into account. Once again, we must insist on the distinctiveness of Biblical faith in doing this. We think in these days of Christian teaching about death and the life to come largely in terms of comfort and consolation, often with the implication that only the weaker, the more unrealistic brethren, either need or are able to find such comfort and consolation. We forget that part of the idea of the Christian tombstone is to be a *memento mori*, a reminder of their mortality to men who would prefer to forget it. Christian faith in the resurrection is no proclamation of 'cheap grace', of automatic entry into eternal bliss for all who find they need such assurance 'as part of the National Health Service'. It is, on the contrary, an assurance that 'the divine comedy' can be seen as such only from beyond tragedy, and that to see it from any other place is to misunderstand it.

All this is gathered up in the Christian interpretation of the Cross. The sense in which it is right to think of Jesus as a tragic

[1] See *Church Dogmatics*, Volume 4 (English translation T. & T. Clark, Edinburgh).

hero needs a great deal of discussion. There has, in fact, been surprisingly little of it in Christian history. That Jesus possessed 'the tragic sense of life', the awareness of man's longing for eternal life in the midst of his sin and mortality, is manifest. That He fulfilled the specification of a tragic hero according to the conventions of Greek tragedy is less clear, partly because of the simple fact that the Greek and the Hebrew universes of discourse were different and complete parallels cannot be drawn. It is also not clear, as far as that goes, that all Greek tragic heroes come within Aristotle's category of being innocent people who are broken on the wheel of fortune. There are points of affinity between Jesus as the suffering servant of Israel and the heroes of Greek tragedy. They both appear to suffer beyond their deserts, are apprehended to be representative in some way of us all and, as far as the Crucifixion, the end appears to be negation. But there are very important differences also.

We may put it like this. Jesus has a very clear recognition of the tragic dimension of existence but He is not adequately thought of as a parallel to the tragic hero of Greece. For He comes *into* the tragic human situation, as one who identifies Himself with the tragic predicament of mankind. He suffers, but He suffers as the servant of God, who sees meaning in His suffering and who is able to make His suffering redemptive. There is pity in the story of Jesus, but the pity is not for Him but for ourselves. 'Daughters of Jerusalem,' he told the women as He went up to the Cross, 'weep not for me but for yourselves and for your children'. (Luke xxiii. 28.) There is terror in the story of Jesus, but the terror again is not that meaningless disaster should overcome us but that, in the presence of the threat of meaninglessness, we should not be found watching with Him. The tragedy, that is to say, is not that of Jesus, but, in the first place, that of Israel, and through Israel of mankind.[1]

---

[1] Israel is like the tragic hero as defined by Aristotle in this sense also, that Israel is neither entirely good nor wholly bad and that what brings about Israel's downfall is a defect of her qualities, her pride in her real religious status and achievements.

He makes us see that, apart from God's peace, our lot is tragic indeed. He does, in one sense, accept the fate of the tragic hero but He is not a typical tragic hero because He accepts this voluntarily. He suffers and goes into the darkness and He dies. Yet His story is not told us in such a way, and therefore we are unable to read it in such a way, that we can regard Him as a tragic figure. To meditate on the cry, 'Is it nothing to you that pass by? See if there be any sorrow like unto my sorrow' is a fitting moment in the following of the Passion story, but it is only a moment. For the man of sorrows who is acquainted with grief has seen of the travail of His soul and is satisfied. This is why the Fourth Gospel is able to tell the story of the Crucifixion as part of the divine comedy, as the exaltation of Christ through suffering and why its effect upon us is not merely that of katharsis but of fulfilment and new zest in living.

It is worth dwelling upon this point for a moment, because it is of great importance. It may seem almost blasphemous to some people to say this but a dramatic tragedy is, after all, only a play. Aristotle's analysis of the effect of tragedy upon the audience can be interpreted as being of a piece with modern 'consumer-research' in its objectivity and, one might almost dare to add, its triviality. But the effect of the Crucifixion upon men is not to enable them to 'have a good cry' and then forget about the matter until the next show comes on. And even if we rightly protest that the actual effect of tragedy, whether Greek or Christian, is much more profound than that, it still falls far short of what the Crucifixion of Jesus Christ does for men. The story of the Crucifixion and Resurrection is not simply a myth, although many mythical elements are caught up with it. It is anchored to history. Jesus Christ 'suffered under Pontius Pilate, was crucified, dead and buried'. In identifying Himself with men in their sin, need and self-contradiction, Jesus gave a dimension to the human tragedy which it has not possessed either before or since.

Why was the death of Christ necessary? This question, which classical statements of the doctrine of the atonement try to answer, lies near the heart of our understanding of the way in which Jesus Christ is related to the 'tragic sense of life'. It was necessary because no less radical way presented itself of making clear the depth of the estrangement between man's actual situation and his true destiny and also the greatness of the loving power of God in decisively overcoming this estrangement. Nothing is further from the truth than the notion, often used as a device by which Jesus is reduced to insignificance, that the Cross was an appendix to His ministry, which took Him by surprise. All the Gospels make clear His recognition that the tragic character of the human predicament meant that He had to fight to the death all that was involved in Israel's rejection of her Lord. He faced and rejected, as we saw in our discussion of the story of His temptation, all other possibilities which presented themselves to Him. He saw that it was necessary that the Son of Man should suffer and die upon the Cross and rise the third day according to the Scriptures because only thus could the full dimension of the human tragedy be made manifest and the grace and favour of God's will towards man, coming from beyond tragedy, be surely based.

This helps us to understand the peculiar quality of the Passion narrative. Those who say that the sufferings and death of Jesus are of significance to us chiefly as an example of how to meet death in a brave, noble and forgiving spirit must find it to be in many ways a serious embarrassment. The history of mankind surely provides better examples of men who met death with composure, dignity and even with humour. The death of Christ is not recounted in a way which is particularly edifying from this point of view. We are not able to say of Him even as we are of the death of Samson that here all passion is spent and that nothing is here for tears, except what quiets us in death so noble. We are confronted with His agony, set in a context of angry conflict, taunts, indignity and betrayal. He dies a convicted criminal, convicted by the properly constituted authorities, and He gives up the Spirit with a loud cry. Men believed that this event was so terrible and awesome that it had repercussions even in the world of nature. 'Now from the sixth hour there was darkness over all the land unto the ninth hour', a darkness followed by an earthquake and strange apparitions.

The reason for this is that Jesus did not go to His death simply as an individual, taking his turn in suffering the common fate of man. He went as representative of Israel, 'the contender with God', as the chief actor in a cosmic drama. He did this, not as a puppet or a lay figure, but with his eyes wide open, apprehending within His mighty Spirit what the full possibilities of life according to the promises of God were and how radical and deadly its denial in sin, evil and death were. Human experience proves that it is possible to treat the approach of death with equanimity, almost with nonchalance, or at least with little more than a spasm of physical fear, if one has treated life as of no significance. Camus' *Outsider* has dramatized this for us. One of the most coldly terrifying things about the executions which follow modern political revolutions is the way in which, if reports are correct, some of their victims treat them as lightly as their executioners. Death ceases to be of much account because life does not add up to much anyway. What has one to lose? The passion of Jesus Christ makes clear that death matters, just as sin matters. It matters because man has eternal life in communion with God to lose. That is why it represents the tragic crisis of human existence.

Most people today do not appear to be as readily conscious as they were, say, in the eighteenth and nineteenth centuries, of the moral burden of their own individual guilt and of the need to know that Christ comes and lifts the burden from them and, covering them with His righteousness, sets them at one again with God. This is not necessarily because we are more enlightened than they but because our consciences have become tired and insensitive, partly because they have been subjected to so many assaults along these lines by professional evangelists equally tired and insensitive. Perhaps, however, our deepened awareness of the pathos, ambiguity and confusion of the general human situation, makes us more ready to see the atoning work of Christ in terms of His bearing the burden of

the 'tragic sense of life' on our behalf, plunging into the abyss
of meaninglessness, which we find intolerable and from which
we recoil, in order to bring it under the control of His Father's
kingdom of order, meaning and life.

It is from this point of view that we can see meaning in His
dereliction and believe, with St. John, that it is when He is
raised up on the Cross that His power to draw all men unto
Him is most clearly revealed. This is possible only after the
event, from beyond tragedy, but from that point of view it
is so revealed and does have that effect on men. This is why
Jesus Christ on the Cross is not simply a tragic figure. He goes
there, not because of error or miscalculation but according to
the determinate counsel and foreknowledge of God, a counsel
and foreknowledge reflected in His own conscious decision as
a man. He bears the full weight of the tragic predicament of
man in His body, the Son of God taking the full impact of the
no-God of this world, as it drives to pull Him with all other
things down into nothingness. But He does this in faith, faith
which, as we have seen, is strong enough even to endure
through the darkness of the dereliction and the three days in
the tomb. He does this as One who, in the strength of His faith,
has chosen to identify Himself with the tragic plight of men,
not as one who is caught and overpowered by it. This is why
we can see Him going up to Jerusalem conquering and to
conquer and why the Church is able to cry, 'Our God is
reigning from the tree'.

This also is why, if we look closely, we see that the resurrection story is told in the Gospels not so much as the overturning
of the Crucifixion as its fulfilment. Indeed, it almost reads like
an appendix to the story of the Passion. To the outward eye,
to the spectator who has followed the events of the ministry
of Jesus afar off, this will not seem to be so. To him the Crucifixion will be the end. As we have seen, the disciples themselves
finally found themselves in that position. But to the Evangelists,
writing after the event and setting it within the context of the
whole ministry of Jesus and, behind that, of the whole history

of Israel, 'according to the Scriptures', it now looks different. The Cross is His triumph and the resurrection is the sign of His triumph and the gift of the Spirit is the seal of His triumph in our lives. Hoskyns and Davey point out the significance here of His rising on the third day.[1] According to Eastern ideas of hospitality, a temporary visit should take three days, the first day a rest day, the second a 'drest' day, when the guest was formally entertained, and the third the day of departure. Anyone who stayed longer was implying that he was no longer a visitor. Similarly, after three days, the body begins to show the ravages of death. But by rising on the third day, Jesus Christ demonstrated that He descended into hell and harrowed it, not as one who belonged there, but as a visitor, staying only long enough to assert His sway over it and to release those imprisoned within it, but returning to the kingdom of life and love where He belonged. The so-called 'ransom' or 'dramatic' account, it can hardly be called a theory, of the atoning work of Christ, which Bishop Aulen has recovered and restated in our own time,[2] is one whose uncompromisingly mythological character strains our weak modern imaginations more than do most parts of theology, but it has the merit of making clear that, in all these events, God through Christ retains the initiative throughout and vindicates His lordship through and beyond tragedy in the revelation.

How can we be sure that this is true and that we are not projecting into this one man's experience our own awareness of moral conflict and hope of its resolution, trying to make another individual's history bear a greater weight than it can possibly be made to bear? In other words, how can we be sure that Christ died for *our* sins and rose for *our* justification? Is it possible for one man to do this for others, especially for others with whom he had no direct personal relationship? This, of course, is the question of the scandal of particularity as it arises with reference to the atoning work of Christ. It is the question

[1] *The Fourth Gospel*, Vol. I, pp. 210–13.
[2] *Christus Victor*, English translation by A. G. Hebert (S.P.C.K., London).

as to whether faith is self-deception which, as we shall continue to see in the rest of our discussion, arises at every point when we consider the meaning of the Christian revelation. The classic Christian answer is that we know the fellowship of Christ's sufferings and the power of His resurrection and we know these in the gift of the Spirit.

What this affirmation of Christian faith means in the context of our understanding of the tragic dimension of human existence is this. When we contemplate the story of the Cross and Resurrection, as though it were a tragic drama, we do not merely find ourselves moved to pity and terror and, as a consequence, to the katharsis of these emotions, so that we can come to some kind of terms with the tragic experience while in essentials it remains the same. On the contrary, in this drama we ourselves are 'existentially' involved. This, in its turn, does not mean simply that we take the initiative in identifying ourselves with the players. The main protagonist Himself draws us into the action. We become the players. It is pity and terror for ourselves and not for the tragic hero which move us and we are not even allowed the katharsis of tears. For at the climax of the action, we make every effort to dissociate ourselves from it. We break out of the theatre, forsaking the protagonist and fleeing, leaving Him to continue with the drama Himself. Yet we find that in doing so, we cannot go away and carry on our lives as we had before we met Him, as though He had never existed except as one of the many who have given a temporary relief to our consciousness of the weary weight of all this unintelligible world. We find that, although we may do our best to forget Him, He does not forget us. He comes into our midst and gives us His peace and breathes upon us with His Spirit. In despite of ourselves, we find that the tragedy has been resolved, that the power of sin and death have been removed, and that we are set free to take our part in God's joyful, life-fulfilling purpose, the divine comedy. The result of this unified dramatic action is not simply the relief of tension produced by the katharsis of our emotions. It is the deliverance expressed in the apostle's 'Be ye, therefore, steadfast, unmoveable, always abounding in the work of the Lord, forasmuch as ye know that your labour is not in vain in the Lord.'[1]

The man who understands that this triumphant affirmation is made only on the basis of a conviction that the resurrection has really happened, will never make it lightly. He will know that it can only come out of an insight into the way in which the Cross deals with the human tragedy. He will see that this kind of conviction is given to men only by God and that it is not for men to be impatient with each other and to start accusing each other when some of them do not seem to have it. But perhaps he is entitled to expect that those who cannot be led to this conviction should make an effort to understand what it is and not try to minimize or by-pass it because they would prefer not to be troubled by it. It remains a surprising fact that there are many people who will not make this effort and who, therefore, fail to come within range of what the Cross and Resurrection really convey to men.

Consider, for example, this apparently sad and moving confession made by Leslie Stephen after the death of his wife, 'Standing by an open grave, and moved by all the most solemn sentiments of our nature, we all, I think—I can only speak for myself with certainty—must feel that the Psalmist takes his sorrow like a man, and as we, with whatever difference of dialect, should wish to take our sorrows; while the Apostle is desperately trying to shirk the inevitable and at best resembles the weak comforters who try to cover up the terrible reality under a veil of well-meant fiction. I would rather face the inevitable with open eyes.' Now this will not do. It will not begin to do. The psalm of which Stephen speaks is presumably the ninetieth psalm quoted in the Burial Service. This speaks

---

[1] I Cor. xv. 58. Or as the N.E.B. puts it, 'Therefore, my beloved brothers, stand firm and immovable, and work for the Lord always, work without limit, since you know that in the Lord your labour cannot be lost.' Love's labour is not lost. We are set free not only to live constructively while bearing the tragic sense of life but also to enjoy life, which can only be done if we see its comedy. Note some illuminating observations on the Christian faith and comedy in *Precarious Vision* by Peter Berger (Doubleday, N.Y., 1961).

most movingly of our mortality, but sets it firmly within the framework of a hymn of praise to God for His faithfulness to men in all generations and a prayer to Him to continue His revealing actions. And St. Paul, again presumably in 1 Corinthians xv, is in no significant sense to be contrasted with the Psalmist. Paul knew the same God as did the Psalmist. He shared the realistic Hebrew attitude towards death. What had confronted him in Jesus Christ was not a comfortable illusion which he strained his mind to believe because it suited his emotional needs to do so. It was a literally blinding reality, which he had found it impossible to avoid or resist. Paul of all men could not be described as a 'weak comforter' and a purveyor of 'well-meant fictions' and if there is anything 'inevitable' which he tried 'desperately' to 'shirk', it was that of acknowledging the lordship of the risen Christ. 'Saul, Saul, why do you persecute me?' (Acts ix. 4.) What drove him to confess the risen Christ, and to believe the testimony of those who had similarly claimed to 'see the Lord', was his own experience of the living Christ as one who was stronger than his own sin and pride and religious zeal and who made sense of his own moral struggles and the history of Israel as no one else did. He met God, the final reality, Yahweh, the God of Israel, in the risen Christ and met Him as the One who had revealed Himself in such a way as to expose and overcome the tragic contradiction of man's nature and give to him a share in His own life.

It is this which prompts Paul to cry out at the end of the great argument in which he has tried to show how Jesus Christ has lifted the burden of sin and healed the tragic rift which runs through all life as we know it, 'If God be for us, who can be against us?' And it is this which gives him the solid conviction that nothing 'in death or life, in the realm of spirits or superhuman powers, in the world as it is or the world as it shall be'[1] can separate us from the love of God in Christ Jesus our Lord. When he asks if 'persecution, hunger, nakedness, peril or sword' are able to make this separation, he is not speaking merely rhetorically, as 'a weak comforter'. He had known these things

[1] Romans viii. 38, 39. N.E.B.

and found that the love of God was with him in the midst. He was able to challenge his readers with these questions because he was confident that the God who had been with him in these extremities would not forsake any others who had known the risen power of Christ. And the ground of his confidence was that that risen power comes from beyond tragedy and gives to those who know it the assurance that nothing is able to overcome it.

CHAPTER IX

The Justification of God

I. Its Characteristic Modern Form

How far have we come at this stage of our argument? We began by trying to see how the question of belief in God was often raised in the wrong context and that it suffered from being discussed in an excessively, or, at least, in an inappropriately academic way. We also tried to emphasize how essential it was to see that the Christian faith in God arose in the dimension of mystery and examined the deficiencies of religious and non-religious ways of denying that this was so. We reminded ourselves of the importance of having an honest and critical attitude in dealing with this fundamental question and the great difficulties in the way of arriving at such an attitude. We considered the so-called traditional proofs of God's existence and tried to revaluate them in the light of the Christian understanding of the relation between revelation and reason. We sought to justify our action in turning away from the great mass of human religion to the Bible as our decisive source for the knowledge of God and in considering what it said, aimed to recapture some of its uniqueness and mystery, which familiarity and inherited preconceptions tend to obscure. We particularly insisted upon the relevance of the knowledge of God possessed by Jesus himself and the prophets and apostles as providing the main evidence for the Christian belief in God, and we considered some of its implications for the understanding of that belief and of human existence in its light. Finally, we examined the question of whether the Christian experience of God could be dismissed as a form of self-deception. We found that it could not and that, indeed, it dealt with the tragic character of human existence more adequately than any other interpretation.

This does not mean, however, that all our questions are now answered. As we have constantly insisted, the issue between faith and unbelief has to be fought all along the line and is never finally resolved in this life. Indeed, to venture out into the life of faith so greatly increases our expectation of joy and fulfilment from life that, in some ways, the difficulties in the way of faith are intensified. The problems discussed in traditional theology under the heading of theodicy, the justification of God to man, do not arise as part of the prolegomena to theology. They arise at a relatively late stage in the discussion, out of the consideration of the doctrine of the Spirit or, alternatively, in relation to eschatology or to God's providential care. They arise for believers, rather than for those outside the circle of faith. They are, as P. T. Forsyth said, part of our concern that God should do justice not merely to our own hopes but to Himself as He has revealed Himself.

The most common form of difficulty which people meet under this head in these days is that of how a God who discloses Himself to be a God of love and who demonstrates the all-conquering power of love in His revelation is yet able to permit an order of things in which there is not merely overt evil, which might be regarded as largely the product of human free will, but also a great deal of apparently innocent and meaningless suffering. It is this which prompts people to say, under the stress of a great public calamity such as an international war, in which they themselves have also suffered deeply, that they have lost their faith. Whatever we may think of such reactions, there can be no doubt that when people see young children being slowly burnt or starved to death or being bombed from the air by their fellow human beings, or those they love being tossed about in the pain of incurable disease or when they read of seemingly pointless natural disasters, such as earthquakes in centres of population, or when they contemplate the apparently aimless and cruel waste which is to be found in the natural order, they are compelled to wonder whether there can be a loving, all-powerful God in control of events.

It is not surprising that this question should have received a great deal of discussion in the modern world, but these considerations to which we now wish to draw attention in the context of our present argument are, however, often ignored. The first is that it is interesting that it is only comparatively recently that this has pressed itself upon the conscience of people as a serious difficulty in the way of Christian belief. The New Testament is curiously uninterested in this difficulty in anything like its modern form. Suffering is certainly a present reality in the New Testament but the suffering of Jesus Christ Himself, which might seem to present the greatest objection to divine existence, is ultimately seen as the reverse. When persecution descends upon the infant church, it is seen, as 1 Peter makes clear, primarily as a trial, a test, of faith, of the kind which believers might reasonably expect. 'My dear friends, do not be bewildered by the fiery ordeal that is upon you, as though it were something extraordinary.' (1 Peter iv. 12, N.E.B.) It is an occasion of sharing in the sufferings of Christ and looking forward to His triumph. Similarly, if the book of Job is looked at carefully, it can be seen that it is not concerned with the problem of suffering in general, as we understand it today. It is about the problems raised by the sufferings of God's righteous servant, Job, whom we can confidently identify with the figure of God's true servant, Israel, who knew calamities enough in the course of her existence. The issue is not 'Why should the innocent suffer?' but rather 'Is God able to vindicate the faith of His servant?' God ironically allows Satan to undertake 'a tempting of God' in order to demonstrate His lordship over against that which appears to contradict it.

When we look at the later history of the Church, right down to the eighteenth century, when the great Lisbon earthquake and the reaction to it may be taken as a convenient landmark, we see a similar curious indifference to the 'problem of suffering' in the terms which have become so familiar today and a much

more robust approach to the whole matter. A striking example
of this is provided by the Order for the Visitation of the Sick
in the Book of Common Prayer of the Church of England.
We wonder how many clergy dare to use it, at least with the
more critical and alert of their members. The Order is not in
the least concerned to reassure the troubled sufferer concerning
God's loving care. It uses the occasion to remind the sufferer
that his end draws near and that his affliction has been sent by
God as a warning. It is only after evidence has been provided
of the sufferer's repentance that anything resembling what we
today would call 'comfort' is offered. Similarly, the Manual of
Olafus Petri, a spiritual directory dating from the days of the
Swedish Reformation, provides advice to the minister about
how to deal with many difficult situations in which people
found themselves in those troubled times. One was that in
which the minister has to speak to an innocent person about to
be hanged. He tells him that although neither he nor the minister knows what sin he has really been guilty of, God does and
that he should accept his punishment like a man.[1] We must
ask ourselves whether all this was due to greater insensitivity
on our fathers' part or whether they saw more in the human
situation in relation to God than most of us do today.

Our second point has been noted more often. It is that the
difficulty of the suffering of the apparently innocent seems to
trouble those who have not themselves suffered very deeply
more than it does those who have. In saying this, we must
hasten to agree that nothing is more unpleasant than the complacent religiosity which confronts the sufferer with the assurance that his sufferings, after all, are part of the will of God and
probably sent to him because of his own sins. Job's friends took
that line and they were decisively rejected. Although, taken out
of context, what Olafus Petri said to the condemned man may
sound like what Job's friends said, this was not really what he
was saying. Christian teaching in relation to suffering operates
in a different dimension of reality from that. It arises out of the
experience of those who have themselves suffered and whose

---

[1] *The Manual of Olafus Petri* (S.P.C.K., London, 1953), pp. 105-7.

sufferings have often arisen as a result of their efforts to fulfil
God's will. It is Job himself, and not his friends, who in the
end is made to cry, 'I had heard of thee by the hearing of the
ear but now mine eye seeth thee, wherefore do I abhor myself,
and repent in dust and ashes'. When Paul cries, 'What shall
separate us from the love of Christ?' and lists a whole series of
calamities as things which might possibly be able to do so, he
was, as we have seen, speaking of things which had happened
to himself. Above all, it is our Lord Himself who, in the
moment of death, is made by the Fourth Gospel to cry, 'Into
thy hands I commend my Spirit', a cry joyfully and with full
assurance echoed in the hearts of countless multitudes of His
followers in their last agony.

The reason for this is that the Christian experience is that,
while suffering is real and its existence does pose a threat to
God's lordship, yet God has come into the midst of human
suffering to show that He has not allowed it to happen through
His own vindictiveness or weakness. He has done this in the
most practical way possible. He has enabled those who trust in
Him to overcome its harmful power in their own lives and to
see ways in which the range of its influence can be progressively
limited, so that they can reasonably hope that one day it will be
finally banished. The fellowship of Christ's sufferings is also
the power of His resurrection. It is this rather than any conventional smugness which prompted the Book of Common
Prayer and *The Manual of Olafus Petri* to take the robust line
which they did, although we might still be left wondering
whether they might not have shown a little more sympathy
with our human weakness. Those who 'know the Lord Jesus
Christ' are sure of one thing, that their suffering is not due to
God's malignancy but to that deep rift in the universe, of which
sin is the expression in the moral sphere, which Biblical tradition calls the 'mystery of iniquity'. They are unable to comprehend this mystery, any more than they can any other,
but, in the light of the Cross and Resurrection, they can see that
God is stronger than it and that the nearer they draw to Him
the more they discover that the dominion of evil over them is

weakened. The dilemma posed by suffering, that if God is all-loving He cannot be all-powerful, and if powerful not all-loving, is irresolvable on the metaphysical level because we, protagonists in the struggle, are not in the place where we can see the end from the beginning. But assurance is given to men which enables them to resolve the dilemma on the practical level, so that they do find it possible to suffer and yet to rejoice in their Saviour's praise, even daring to count it a privilege to share with Him a little of the burden which He bore for our redemption. To the outsider, who does not know the fellowship of the sufferings of Christ, this will carry no conviction[1] and even to those Christians who have not suffered much its mysterious character will be much in evidence. They will never speak of it lightly and will see the need to pray that grace will be given them to behave in this way if they are called upon to suffer. But those who have been driven by the force of suffering into the secret place of the most High testify that it is here, more than anywhere, that they abide under the shadow of the Almighty. Their suffering, like any deep experience, quickens their apprehension of the real nature of things. This leads them to see the reality of God and His kingly rule and thus to overcome that threat of meaninglessness, deeper than all pain, which is the greatest terror of suffering.[2]

[1] 'It belongs to the unredeemed sinful state of man, it forms part of the punishment of sin, that man cannot solve the theodicy problem—unless he repents and believes. Indeed, the theodicy problem finally proves to be a form of unbelief, in so far as man allows himself to adopt the role of an objective, neutral spectator, in so far, that is, as the question is raised from a point outside one's own responsibility . . . and man pretends that he is the judge (theodike), when man really stands in the dock before the heavenly Judge. It is not for God to justify Himself, but it is He who judges and justifies us through Jesus Christ the crucified, through whom He reveals to us both our guilt and His almighty mercy.' From E. Brunner, *Dogmatic*, Vol. II, p. 183. This must indeed be true, but none of us can be so strong in faith as to be able to recognize its truth in any other way than with fear and trembling. This is a point at which we have always to arrive, never one from which we can confidently start, in dealing with suffering.

[2] Our claim is not that all suffering does this. Suffering can sometimes be so great as to weaken the apprehension, but it remains significant that in so far

We can also go on to say, although even more humbly and tentatively, that they can go on to console themselves with the thought that what they know to be true for themselves in their own experience cannot be altogether untrue even for those in whose sufferings outsiders can see little or no meaning. Here, above all other places, believers will be cautious to avoid even an appearance of rushing in to justify God's ways, as though His honour depended upon their ability to give a satisfactory explanation of His inscrutable providence. We cannot see the end from the beginning even in our own internal lives, still less in the calamities which befall others. Life confronts us with many dark places and the way of honesty, and therefore of faith, is often simply to confess that the darkness is too deep for us to penetrate. Yet if we know Christ's light in our own darkness, we can hold fast to Him and believe that He is present in the darkness of others also. We can, at least, point them through the darkness to His cross, which would be completely invisible were it not for the light of the resurrection behind it.

The issue presented by the suffering of the apparently innocent is a real one for faith and, in these days when men have developed unparalleled power for inflicting suffering upon each other and almost equally unparalleled self-righteousness in justifying themselves for doing so on the basis of their ideologies, it is important that the issue be kept alive. Nowhere is sanctimonious complacency more inappropriate than here and old-fashioned religion, Protestant and Catholic alike, has too often been guilty of it. Yet to see the issue of theodicy in terms only or even chiefly of the problems created by the suffering of the apparently innocent is to show a lack of awareness of the full dimension of the issue which may be one of the chief barriers in the way of achieving its resolution. It is true that it is a sign of the decline of moral insight rather than its growth when people become more preoccupied with questions of pain and suffering and their avoidance than with those of justice and

as it sharpens the apprehension, this is the characteristic thing which it makes suffering Christians say. It would be impertinent for anyone who has not suffered as they have to dismiss their testimony as illusory.

righteousness. This has its analogy in the attitude which is more
concerned with the well-being of the criminal than with the
protection of the rest of society from him and with redress for
his victims. It needs to be emphasized that this is indeed the
defect of a precious quality, but it is a defect none the less. It
owes as much to modern individualism and moral scepticism
as it does to a refinement of the sense of justice and of fellow-
feeling. This is why P. T. Forsyth put the question in a more
constructive context when he said, in a book written in the
height of the grim and desperate First World War, 'We think
and worship as if the only question was whether God loved us,
instead of whether His love has absolute power to give itself
eternal and righteous effect.'[1]

II. Does God Vindicate Himself in Human History?

It is in this form that the question concerning theodicy has
most actively troubled the minds of believers, both in Biblical
times and until the development of characteristically modern
self-consciousness. At the heart of the Christian message stands
the assertion that Jesus Christ has decisively broken the power
of that which denies God, the sign of which victory is His
resurrection. Through the universalization of His power, expressed in the Ascension, and through the gift of the Spirit,
God's victorious might is available to men. The purpose of His
coming was to re-establish God's kingly rule in the life of men
and their world. When He said 'the kingdom of God is in your
midst', He did not simply mean that it was an inward and
personal kingdom, He meant that it was now present as an
active reality in the midst of this life. Through Him, the powers
of the age to come, when God shall be all in all, are now
operative in our midst and we have access to them. Whether
we believe or not that C. H. Dodd's way of describing the
eschatological teaching of the New Testament as 'realized' or

[1] *The Justification of God* (Duckworth, London, Charles Scribner, N. Y.,
1917), p. 3.

'inaugurated' is the best that can be achieved, it has the un-
doubted merit of calling proper attention to something which
was at the heart of the apostolic preaching, and which also
controlled the life of the apostolic community. As Paul said,
'Weak men we may be, but it is not as such that we fight our
battles. The weapons we wield are not merely human, but
divinely potent to demolish strongholds.' (2 Cor. x. 3-4,
N.E.B.) And we are able to do this because of the 'vast resources
of the power' which are open to those who trust in God. These
can be measured only by his (God's) 'strength and might which
he exerted in Christ when he raised him from the dead, when
he enthroned him at his right hand in the heavenly realms, far
above all government and authority, all power and dominion,
and any title of sovereignty that can be named, not only in this
age but in the age to come. He put everything in subjection
beneath his feet, and appointed him as supreme head to the
church, which is his body and as such holds within it the fullness
of him who himself receives the entire fullness of God.' (Eph. i,
19-23, N.E.B.)

Now it is true that the Bible never implies for a moment
that, once the resurrection has happened and the Spirit has been
shed abroad, all evil and conflict will disappear. A large part of
the second letter to the Corinthians in which the first of our
quotations appears, is taken up with a long cry of agony and
frustration on the apostle's part in the presence of evil and
failure, even on the level of elementary understanding, in the
heart of the newly-born church itself. Evil, and sin, will continue to flaunt themselves for a season, although their power of
final resistance has been broken. Their 'doom is writ', in the
words of Luther's hymn, but it is not yet completely established.
Theologians and preachers, anxious to make clear the situation,
have been disposed since the Second World War to use the
analogy of the situation of the Allied armies between the
successful launching of the D-Day invasion and V-Day. The
enemy has still a great deal of fight left in him and can inflict
many casualties but we know, and in the end he knows, that
he has no chance. The morale of his home base has been shat-

tered and the forces ranged against him are demonstrably more powerful than he can overcome.

The analogy may, or may not, be a helpful one, but it certainly does not serve to remove the 'theodicy' difficulty from our minds. Let it be agreed that, to continue with this slightly tiresome military metaphor, we are still in the period of 'mopping-up operations' and that these can be painful and costly. We continue to need to be assured that there is movement towards finality. Christ's kingdom must be in process of becoming more and more visible among men. The power of evil must be more and more exposed in its self-contradiction and futility. The fruit of the Spirit in love, joy and peace should be shed abroad more and more freely in the life of this world. We might recognize that all this cannot happen by simple progression. Life, like warfare, is too tangled-up and untidy for that. Often it will seem as pointless and incoherent as the Battle of Waterloo did to the youth in *The Charterhouse of Parma* who was caught up in it without realizing that it was the Battle of Waterloo. But, taking the long view, Christ's kingdom should be asserting its reality ever more fully in this life if the Christian claim is to have any validity. Is this happening? Or is what is happening that, with the continuing delay in the coming of the Parousia, the Christian movement is losing its impetus and proving itself to be, after all, no more than one movement among others in the story of men, one of the 'little systems' which 'have their day and cease to be', so that we need henceforward to look elsewhere for real redemptive power in the life of men?

Delay in the coming of the Day of the Lord, often closely connected with a particular crisis in the life of the nation, was something which constantly troubled the men of the Old Testament, especially in the prophetic period. The psalms are full of this. 'Lord, how long' is one of their most characteristic cries. 'We have heard with our ears, our fathers have told us', men in Israel said, 'what mighty deeds thou didst in their days, the days of old.' These were the days of the deliverance from Egypt and the journey to the Promised Land, but now it looked

as though the Lord's hand was shortened that it could not save
and His ear heavy that it could not hear. The Psalmist has seen
the wicked in great power and spreading himself like a green
bay tree, or like a tree that grows in its own soil, flourishing as
though in its natural habitat (Ps. xxxvii. 35). And he is confronted by the heathen, who taunt him with the question,
'Where is thy God?' since, as far as eye can see, He is not at
work in the world. And, as we have seen, Job's question was
essentially one concerning God's ability to vindicate His
covenant with Israel.

The psalmists and the prophets were sustained primarily by
the hope that the day of the Lord would yet come, when the
King would be truly exalted. They saw the enthronement of
the King in Israel as an eschatological pre-figurement of Yahweh's final coming, when He would judge the world with
righteousness and His peoples with His truth. With the intensification of their national situation, this eschatological expectancy took a more apocalyptic form and they began to look
increasingly for the appearance of one like unto the Son of
Man, to whom would be given dominion and glory and a
kingdom. But according to Christian faith, that day came. The
Messianic prophecies were fulfilled and Yahweh established His
universal kingdom in Jerusalem, reigning, in the paradox of
His love for sinful men, from the tree of crucifixion outside
the wall of the city. The Word became flesh and dwelt among
us, and we beheld His glory. Salvation was granted to mankind
and the powers of the age to come were made available to us
in the Spirit, and the claim was made that they were stronger
than the principalities and powers. It is true that there was a
continuing 'apocalyptic' element in the New Testament but
part of the reason for it lay not so much in dissatisfaction with
the first Coming as in an intensification of awareness of the way
in which all things were moving to their final resolution under
the impetus of what had already been accomplished in Jesus.
Perhaps the dominating note of the New Testament, is that
the kingdom is already an active, present reality in the midst
and that it is destined to reach its fulfilment when all things are

brought under the sway of Christ. The first half of Christian eschatology is the event of the cross and resurrection. The second half, following on from the exaltation of the risen Christ through the Ascension, is only partly a second Coming of Christ in a different form from that in which we now know Him. It is also, as J. A. T. Robinson says, 'for John, the person and work of the Paraclete, who takes the things of Jesus and makes perfect in us his presence of love. It is, for the Epistle to the Hebrews, the perpetual intercession of the Priest-King, appearing henceforward within the veil on our behalf. It is, in Pauline terms, the Body of Christ, into which all is being brought, "by that power which enables him even to subject all things to himself".' (Phil. iii. 21.)[1] We may believe, more definitely than Robinson suggests, that these point to a final decisive event but they also to some extent already partake of its nature.

The life of the Christian community must not be thought of primarily as that of watching and waiting for the end of all things. It must be that of being conformed to the sphere of life whose nature has been revealed in Jesus Christ, by the means which He has appointed, through the Spirit in the Body on the basis of His perpetual intercession. It lives by the tokens of His appearing, by the presence in the midst of this present age, which is 'passing away to nothingness', of the abundant life, the life which is life indeed, which Jesus Christ has brought. The reality of His coming must vindicate itself, not by the establishment of a second Parousia at a particular time and place—that is to misunderstand the nature of His real coming—but by bringing forth the fruit of the Messianic kingdom.

This is the claim of the New Testament, and it is at this very point that some of the most searching and persistent criticism of Christian faith arises, the more searching, as always, because it arises out of expectations aroused by some understanding and experience of what God's promise to Abraham and his seed implies. It has always been the main objection of that Judaism which continues to be informed with Biblical concreteness and

[1] *Jesus and His Coming* (S.C.M. Press, London, 1957), p. 183.

realism that the claim of Jesus Christ is not true because the prophecies have not been fulfilled and the Messianic kingdom has not been inaugurated. According to Judaism, the world goes on very much as it did before the coming of Jesus Christ. Similarly, Communism, with its frequently noted apocalyptic strain, dismisses Christianity on the grounds that it is ineffective, except as an opiate which prevents people from bestirring themselves so as to participate in the real events of revolutionary activity. And in modern times, many ordinary people have reached more or less the same conclusion, although in a more easy-going and tolerant way. 'Christianity', they say, 'is a fine ideal, but it doesn't work out in practice.' The implication of this is that it is well-meaning but ineffective. If the evil is not necessarily stronger than the good, at least the good as it has been expressed in Jesus Christ and His Spirit, does not appear to have any special power of being able, in the sense intended by the New Testament itself, 'to overcome the world'.

This attitude of dissatisfaction, bordering upon disillusionment, with the apparent delay in the fulfilment of the kingdom is also found, however, among people of much more serious intent, who are passionately concerned that something they identify with the kingdom should come into being. Many people feel this about world peace in the nuclear age. They echo the words of Joan of Arc in Charles Péguy's play of that name, 'O God, if only the beginning of your kingdom would come. If only the sunrise of your kingdom would come. But there is nothing, nothing to see, ever. You sent your Son, whom you loved so much, your Son came, who suffered so much, and He died, and there is nothing, nothing ever. If only we could see the dawn of your kingdom beginning to break. And you sent your saints, and you called them each by name, and your saints came, and nothing, nothing ever. Years went by, so many years that I do not know how many there were; centuries of years went by; fourteen centuries of Christendom, alas! since the birth, and the death and the preaching. And nothing, nothing ever. And what reigns on the face of the earth is nothing, nothing, nothing but perdition. . . . God, God, can it be that your Son died in vain? That He came, and it was all for nothing?'[1]

In less intense and less rhetorical form, this question has been asked by many people in the years since the birth and the death and the preaching. We must not be put off from asking it by the fact that it is often expressed, as it is in this quotation from a French play, in an extreme and exaggerated way. The exaggeration is certainly often present in these protests. Even to the most superficial observer, and, as we shall see, superficial observation is not likely to take us very far in dealing with this particular matter, it is not true to say that nothing has changed on earth because of the coming of Christ. The Christian Church in its various institutional manifestations is an ambiguous enough organization but, to put it at its lowest, it has had a considerable influence on human history, not all of it evil. It is true that the Christian community has had its ups and downs. One of the reasons for the prevalence of the popular notion that Christianity is a fine ideal which does not work out in practice is the fact that churches have themselves been too ready in recent generations to win public approval, or at least acquiescence, at the price of cheapening and trivializing their message. But there are plenty of examples in the last two thousand years to show that Christian faith does work and exercises a transforming and reconciling power in men's lives. One of our difficulties also is that, under the influence of latter-day Christian romanticism, we have become accustomed to look for the fruit of the Spirit in the wrong places and are disappointed when we fail to find it. We have inclined to assume that Christian action must be heroic, spectacular and dramatic, lending itself readily to use as illustrative material in sermons, and have overlooked the fact that real change and real growth only rarely take these striking forms, and are much more commonly slow, halting and painful, in the way in which change and growth generally are. Their significance also is generally visible only after the lapse of a good deal of time, or when they are viewed from some distance.

[1] See *Péguy and les Cahiers*, p. 98 by Daniel Halévy, p. 99 (Dennis Dobson, London, 1946).

The Justification of God

The influence of Christian faith upon our lives may be more fundamental in the things which we take for granted, in our way of looking at the world, our dogmas in T. E. Hulmes' sense, than in our formal beliefs and in our conscious decisions. When we see this, the difference which it makes may be more striking than appeared to be the case at first sight. Professor Cochrane's book on Christianity and Classical Culture has indicated what a transformation of outlook the coming of the Christian faith achieved in the ancient world and if an objective comparison were possible between life in the Anglo-Saxon democracies of the modern world which have strong Christian influences at work in them and life in countries which lack such influences, it might be that similar differences would emerge.

The last thing we should want to imply is that this provides anyone with cause for self-congratulation. The difference which the coming of Christ has made is one which intensifies the human situation, and this can force out the evil in men to become more overt as well as the good. The experience of Germany in the years between the wars proves the truth of this. Nor do we wish to try to produce a catalogue of achievements to be set down to the credit of the more-or-less Christian nations. That is clearly as impossible as it is unreal and not the way in which a Christian who knows that all his righteousnesses are but as filthy rags before the Lord should ever think of acting. But Christians have been driven by their own experience to the conviction that the coming of Christ makes a real difference to men's lives and they are entitled to maintain that it is not true to say out of hand that it has made none, or that what it has made is insignificant. For good or for ill, it has undoubtedly made a great deal of difference. The real questions are these. Has it made enough to justify the great claims which it makes for itself? Or, if that is not the right way to put it, since these questions certainly cannot be properly answered in purely quantitative terms, is there a way of looking at life which enables the Christian to find assurance of faith as he contemplates the issues of human affairs? The quality and the sufficiency of the fruit we bring forth is known ultimately only to God.

But we need at least to know that some fruit exists. And we need much more to be able to know that God's hand is at work in the world and that His purpose of love is still moving forward.

III. The Christian View

The question of whether God vindicates Himself in history must always present its challenge to faith and, as we shall see, it can never be answered once for all, so that we need no longer be troubled by any difficulties in relation to theodicy. Yet here, as always, we can help ensure that we are, at least, posing the question properly, in such a way that we may reasonably expect an answer, by a more careful consideration of the manner in which the men of the Bible approached it.

It is not easy for us to do this because their conception of time and of history was, in important respects, different from our own. The New Testament conception of time has been the subject of a good deal of scholarly investigation and scholars have come up with different conclusions.[1] The subject is a complex one but, fortunately for our present purpose, we need do no more than note two of the different ways in which the men of the Bible thought of time. They thought of it both chronologically and, as it has been described, realistically. Two words used in the New Testament make clear the difference, chronos and kairos. The first means ordinary duration, in which one moment is exactly like the next, a unit of time, measurable, external and neutral. It is time looked at from the outside, made use of by man to order and check his life. Kairos, however, is time subjectively considered, looked at from the inside in relation to the development of human purposes. When

[1] See O. Cullmann, *Christ and Time*, and John Marsh, 'Time' in the *Theological Word Book of the Bible* and his book *The Fulness of Time* (Nisbet, London). See also a criticism of both these writers in J. Barr, *Biblical Words for Time*. (S.C.M. Press, London). See too K. Barth *Church Dogmatic*, Vol. 3. 2, pp. 437–640.

any particular kairos is upon us, a particular series of events in chronological time is fulfilled, time has been transformed into history. The coming of Christ was supremely a kairos, a fulfilment of the history of Israel, through which all that had gone before could now be understood. As their understanding of its implications developed, the apostolic church also went on to say that it was also a kairos in relation to what came after it, determining its shape and giving it its meaning. The coming of the kairos does not mean that chronological time is abolished. It remains as it did, although even here the kairos provides it with its point of reference, the place of vantage from which we are able to order chronological time creatively and with meaning. (Even chronological time since the coming of Christ is divided into B.C. and A.D.) But all that happens in chronologically measurable time is now decisively affected by this kairos.

We can put this in another way by saying that in the Cross and Resurrection, which takes place in the setting of chronological time, as all human activity does, God has shown us that which enables us to interpret all our kairoi, no matter when in chronological time we may happen to live. This is not simply another way of saying what many people have said, that the story of Jesus Christ is a particularly striking illustration of certain general principles which can be deduced from the study of human history and the universe around us. Christ's work is a unique event, the fruit of God's personal intervention in human affairs. But it has significance not only for the moments in which it actually took place but also for what came after and, no less, for what went before. Sin, suffering and death remain in the world since His death and resurrection as they did before. This is manifest and to suggest that the Christian faith ever implied anything different is not only to fly in the face of what it says but also to maintain that from the beginning Christians were deluded fools who were unable to look a plain fact in the face. Sin, suffering and death remain in the world but the Cross and Resurrection show them both to be very powerful and yet not powerful enough to affect the final destiny of God's creation. Evil has been overcome at the heart of the universe, in the ultimate trial of strength, and God's purpose of love is what will finally triumph. The Cross and the Resurrection are not in themselves the end of all things, but they are a revelation of the end. They indicate how things will finally work out, but they also do more. Because they are a genuine revelation, they also help us to see both how things have worked out in the past and also how to have our part in the way in which things are working out now and will continue to work out according to God's purpose. This is the strength of the Biblical conviction of election and the secret of the continuing power of Calvinist theology, even though we may agree that Calvinism does not always succeed in drawing out the right implications from the conviction of election. The tokens we possess of the authenticity of the cross and resurrection are more than the testimony of the 'eye-witnesses of His majesty' to His risen reality. They are also those derived from our own possession of the Spirit, 'the pledge of our inheritance', re-presenting Christ to us and leading us into all the truth.

As we have already seen from several points of view, the very fact that the Cross and Resurrection give an insight into the final destiny of all things also provides the basis for our action here and now in the midst of this 'age which passes away'. It means that we can live as those who are 'in' but not 'of' this age but who can infuse this age with the glory of the age which is to come and whose power is already available to us. It is only when it has become distorted and misunderstood that Christian eschatological expectation inhibits creative action in this life. In itself, it provides the impetus and the means by which we can express something of the joy and vitality of the eternal kingdom here and now. But, again as always in the Christian life, the two sides of the event which determines our existence must always be held together. Our life is one of the fellowship of Christ's sufferings and of the power of the resurrection, and it cannot truly be the one without also being the other. The power of sin is still present in our midst and we have to wrestle with it as our Lord in His humanity did. We find it in our own hearts and we are caught in a network of sinful relationships.

The Justification of God

We are men of unclean lips and we dwell in the midst of a people of unclean lips. The very fact that we have had a vision of our Lord, high and lifted up, drives that home to us. Yet the same vision itself also makes power available to overcome that sin. It exposes the ultimate unreality, the lack of ability to establish itself permanently, which that sin has and it gives us the confidence to go forward to live by the law of Christ's kingdom of righteousness and love in the midst of a sinful world. This is true even in those decisions where the influence of sin is most pervasive and where we are caught in situations where evil has to be endured or condoned. We can limit the range of the evil, we can prevent it from spreading and we can surround it with the healing power of Christian love. It is possible also to behave in a similar way in the presence of death. Death remains a factor in life, as it was from the beginning. Yet the vision of the end we have in Christ assures us that the last word is not with death. The most remarkable characteristic of the New Testament on the subject of death is its reticence, a reticence not always shown by those who claim to speak in its name. We do not know what happens beyond the grave. But we do know the power of the resurrection, and this enables us to face the fact of having to die in its full magnitude and yet to have the courage to live and to fall asleep in Jesus Christ when our time comes, with our souls resting in hope.

When life is looked at from this point of view, all the difficulties which confront Christian theodicy are not removed, but at least a good deal of the ground is cleared, so that it can be seen more precisely where the real difficulties lie. The last thing the believer expects is to have to live in a perfect world where he does not need to encounter evil, sin and suffering. These have not been abolished nor have they been shown to be of no account. His life consists in a struggle with them and his faith, illumined by the Cross, has shown him how strong and how pervasive they are. But his faith has also shown him that these can be overcome. They are unreal in the sense that they do not have the ability to sustain themselves indefinitely but are ultimately self-defeating. He knows this because Christ has demon-

186

strated it in dealing with the sin which confronted Him on this earth and it is this which gives him the confidence to approach his neighbour and the world around him in the conviction that perfect love casteth out fear. Sin and its consequences can never, while we remain on this earth, be left out of account or defeated once for all. They constantly appear and reappear in the changing circumstances of life and the believer has to be ceaselessly vigilant against them. But this is not the same as saying that the terms of the struggle between grace and sin remain unchanged from age to age. Faith has always to revindicate its reality in the face of its contradiction, but there is a measure of progress even in its acts of revindication.

The progress is certainly not one which can be traced in a continuous line from an ordinary human point of view, as though we had one rational principle at work in relation to another in a static situation. Sin is irrational and no one knows where it will next break out and, as we have said, the whole battle-field presents a much more untidy picture than that. Further, for us to be able to see the total picture of the way the battle is going would mean that we are above it, which we are not. This is why it will frequently seem to us, in our part of the field, that we may have lost and it will often need a great deal of faith on our part to be able to repeat the familiar cliché with any degree of meaning, that we have lost a battle but not the war. Yet faith seeking understanding will be able to see, from time to time, that the power of God is effectively at work and is proving itself stronger than its opponents. The spiritual conflict is not one where a tie or a stalemate is possible. Good and evil are not equally poised. The good is stronger than the evil. In the world in which Jesus Christ has risen from the dead, the chances of good rather than evil prevailing in any situation, other things being equal, are not less than 51 to 49. There is at least that much truth in the 'power of positive thinking'. The true believer does not believe that 'the universe is on his side', that the stars in their courses are fighting for him. He knows enough about himself to see, as the Psalmist did not always manage to see, that his side is never unambiguously that of the angels. But he does believe that the universe is on the side of the good. It is not utterly cold and indifferent, even though the good does not yet have all its own way with it. He sees this, not because we yet see all things brought into subjection unto Him but because we do see Jesus, crowned with glory and honour, and seeing Him, know that good is more real than evil, even as being is than non-being. This is why, knowing that he is still imperfect, that he has not attained to the resurrection of the dead which he has seen in Jesus, the believer is able to forget the things which are behind—the old life in which he lay under the dominion of sin—and to stretch forward to the things which are before, to press on to the goal, to the prize of the high calling of God in Jesus Christ. This is not his present possession, over which he has control and which, therefore, could confirm him in his pride, but it determines the whole set of his life in the midst of his present imperfection.

There must be spiritual progress in the fulfilment of God's purpose if Christian faith is to vindicate itself in history, and the man of faith must seek and find assurances that God's spirit is active in the affairs of men. He will realize that these assurances can only be given from the point of view of faith. That does not mean any diminution of their reality, it means that they can be seen and properly evaluated only when a man is looking at them in a certain light, that shed by revelation in Jesus Christ Himself. This carries with it implications about the places where we should look for such assurances. They will be likely, for example, to emerge much more clearly from our understanding of our internal lives and our direct relationship with other people than from our understanding of public events and the life of institutions. It is in the personal dimension that grace most freely operates and where its antithesis is most readily recognized and shown to be the destructive force which it is. When we move into the realm of the operation of institutions, several other complicating factors enter in. All institutional forms are subject to the law of this world which passes away and the more they are 'objectified' the more completely is this so. This is true of the Church as an institution among others in the world. Indeed, the nature of the Church as an institution is such, owing to the irresistible drive of religious organizations towards conservative defensiveness in the absence of the Spirit, that it could be argued that this is particularly true of the Church. This is why it is essential that the Church should always strive to distinguish sharply between herself and her Lord. Churches, and other religious organizations, are born, grow, flower, bear fruit, wither and decay, like any others, although some of them may seem to take an unconscionably long time a-dying. The fact that churches and religious movements have their ups and downs is, therefore, in itself no argument against the reality of the divine movement in history. It would be a powerful argument if this were the whole story and churches never showed signs of breaking forth into new life and finding renewal and reformation. There are some churches which show this lack of vitality especially, although not only, in places around the shores of the Mediterranean, and their existence in this form does constitute a challenge to faith. But what constitutes the assurance that God has not forsaken His people is that there does seem to be, in most instances, a bush which burns and is not consumed at the heart of the Church's life, which compels men to turn aside again to see and to know once more the Lord's deliverance. It does happen time and time again, and often in the most unexpected places, that when the outer man of the Church is dying, the inner man is renewed. And it is a renewal which has learnt something fresh from the decay which has overtaken the old man.

It is wrong to say that there has been development in the life of the Christian community since apostolic times in the sense that we have been able to add anything of significance to the essential content of the Gospel or in the sense that the faith of men today is stronger and deeper than that of the apostolic church. But there has been development in the sense that more and more of the meaning of the great events of our redemption and of God's purpose for the world stands revealed. There has been development also in the sense that Christ's redemptive power has been put to the test by being transplanted into radically different cultures and historical situations and ranges of experience from those known in Biblical times and has come through the test. Men have found in their own experience and through observation of their neighbours and even, more brokenly, in the life of institutions and communities, that a little leaven of true faith is able to spread through the whole lump and that faith as of a grain of mustard seed, provided it is authentic, is able to move mountains.

There has been progress also in the sense that it seems to become clearer that, as time goes on, the principalities and the powers, the demons which rule men's lives, become increasingly less effective, or at least find it increasingly difficult to sustain their grip over men for any length of time. By the principalities and powers we may mean, following Barth, all those supra-individual combinations of notions and sentiments which are given a quasi-personal identity by men and treated as belonging to an order of divinity. In our own time we can think of Reason, Science, the Nation, the Classless Society, Sex, the British Monarchy, the American Way of Life, Private Enterprise, and many other semi-realities. In this sense, the principalities and powers, with the 'images' they present, are as active today as they have ever been. What is significant about them in our own time, however, is the shortness of the lease on life which each of them appears to hold. They may indeed grip men with a great intensity but the very intensity has a despairing quality which indicates a basic lack of confidence. It is hard for idols to maintain themselves in the modern world. They are far more vulnerable to the 'acids of modernity' than is faith. This is most obviously true in the case of the political idols but a prophet has already begun to document 'the decline and fall of sex'.[1] This vulnerability is one of many reasons why churchmen should not try to make deals with the principalities and powers in the hope of using their apparent strength to buttress that of the triune God. Such deals, common enough as they are in the history of churches, are implicit denials of the fact that we live in a world where the Resurrection has already happened and

[1] See the book of that title by Robert M. Fitch (Harcourt, Brace, New York)

where we can already begin to enter into the inheritance of the Messianic kingdom. If Bonhoeffer's protest against 'religion' is taken as a protest against the principalities and powers, including those which wear Christian masks, it is timely indeed. The more mature Christian faith becomes, the more it expresses in this life that which is the eternal fulfilment of the purpose of God, the more religionless in this sense it must become.

The necessity to remember this becomes more pronounced when it is also recognized that the New Testament insists that the evil, as well as the good, ripens unto the day of judgment. Bernard Manning, an English historian of conservative temper, once observed that the only 'progressives' mentioned in the Bible were the Gadarene swine. In this he was wrong, since he chose to overlook the fact, strangely in one who claimed to stand in the succession of the Pilgrim Fathers, that the whole Christian life was conceived of as a pilgrimage, moving forward to the Promised Land. But the remark does remind us that the evil as well as the good is driven by its own inherent logic to its fulfilment, which in this case is self-destruction. It is important to see that the good and the evil ripen together. The warmth of the Sun of righteousness brings out the inherent quality of the evil in the same way as it does the good. The crucifixion itself conclusively demonstrates this. In the presence of the good, the nature of the evil is made peculiarly vivid, and its destructive power operates the more speedily. We have seen this also in our own time. Evil in those lands where the Christian gospel has been preached and where, despite their best efforts, men have never been able entirely to get its sound out of their ears is nearly always more savage, hysterical and cruel than in lands where men have not been stabbed by it into a high degree of self-consciousness. The only consolation we have in such a situation is that particular manifestations of evil burn themselves out the more quickly and are more short-lived. Modern Germany is a country whose history most pitifully bears this out. In the world of today, however, where Christian insight and technological advance are making us realize the ecumenical nature of the society of men, we must realize that evil will also be present on the ecumenical level, ripening with the good. This is a sign of the imminence of the Judgment. The frenzy of evil and the dreadful consequences which it can bring with it, of which we are acutely aware today, are not a sign of the unreality of the Gospel. They are the inevitable negative consequence of rejection of the Gospel and a warning to us all of the urgent need for vigilance and repentance.

It is not always clear from the teaching of Jesus about the judgment as to whether He was referring to His own Cross and Resurrection or to an event which would follow them. The probability is that, as with the Parousia, He was referring to His Cross and Resurrection as expressions in terms of this life of a final event. Where Christ comes, there is the judgment, but it is a judgment which is not yet completely fulfilled in all its implications. Now is the judgment of the world and now the prince of this world is cast out, and we can only live in this present age in accordance with that judgment, but that judgment is not manifest to all. It has to be discerned and acknowledged in the presence of that which still proudly tries to defy it. We have to discover the judgment of the Lord in the ever-changing circumstances of life and we can only do so if, as the collect for Whit Sunday in the Book of Common Prayer says, we have the gift of charity, which is the human reflection of the divine judgment and which alone enables us in our turn to have a right judgment in all things. The reason for this is given us very clearly in the familiar passage from the Fourth Gospel where we are told that our Advocate, who is the Spirit, will show us where wrong and right and judgment lie. 'He will convict them of wrong, by their refusal to believe in me; he will convince them that right is on my side, by showing that I go to the Father when I pass from your sight; and he will convince them of divine judgment, by showing that the Prince of this world stands condemned.'[1]

This happens now, yet as it does so the Spirit is pointing forward to the fulfilment of His work. The day will come when the human possibility of refusing to give heed to the judgment of

[1] John xvi, 9–11 (N.E.B.).

the Lord will no longer be open to us. We shall be called to our
final account, with no space left open for repentance. When this
will be we are not told. Once again, the economy and the reserve
of the most characteristic portions of the New Testament stand
out. But the nature of the divine reality which we know in our
present experience of His judgments in the Spirit is such as to make
us see that our only hope in the final judgment is to trust in the
Lord's righteousness and mercy, whose nature has been decisively
revealed in the Cross and Resurrection. The day of the Lord is
now always at hand, breaking in upon us. The kingdom, the
kingly rule of God is in the midst, as a present reality governing
all our actions. Those in the Early Church who thought chiefly
in terms of the final consummation coming in their own life
were misled into thinking in chronological terms of something
which belongs to another order of reality but they were not
wrong in thinking of the End as an urgent reality which we
have to take into account in all our present calculations. This is
poles apart from the smug piety which qualifies its announce-
ments of little routine events with the letters D.V., or 'the Lord
willing'. It recognizes that the terms upon which life is to be
lived henceforward are clear enough, whether its consummation
is near or far chronologically speaking, and that it is for us to
get on with the job of living it. We are the community of those
who have been given a little time by God in which to participate
in His active work of reconciliation and healing, while we wait
with 'eager expectation' for the fulfilment of all things in Christ.

This understanding of the situation of the community of faith
helps us to see meaning in its present life and to give direction
for its future action. It does not claim to explain the fact of
continuing evil. No general interpretation of why there should
be continuing evil in the world is possible, any more than a
completely adequate account of the origin of evil is possible.
This is not to say that all attempts to provide such interpretations are wrong or misleading. It is right to look into the
mystery of iniquity as it is into the mystery of God and of being
itself. To say, for instance, that it arises as a possibility inherent
in the gift of free will is not to say nothing even though it is

not to say very much. But ultimately, perhaps, the most rationally constructive thing we can say about evil in general is that, from our ordinary human point of view, it is inexplicable. It is the basic irrationality of the universe, the absurd, but the absurd in a tragic rather than a comic way. Evil is that which contradicts meaning. Faith cannot explain it but at least faith can see why it cannot explain it. And in seeing why it cannot explain it, faith discovers also that it is able to deal with it. For faith discovers as it encounters each recurring manifestation of evil that as it looks upon evil 'in Jesus Christ', it is able to expose its irrationality, its stupidity, and in so doing, to draw its sting from it. By the grace of God, faith is able, at least, to name the demons and that is sufficient, on the level of our fragmentary human encounters, temporarily to break their spell over us. As the myth of Satan, who is 'the father of lies', indicates, our knowledge of evil comes from the same dimension as our knowledge of the good and this means that our situation is such that we can only conquer it in each encounter as we meet it, walking by faith and not by sight. But it is possible to conquer it and to expose, with ever-increasing clarity, its emptiness and futility.

It is with this that the man of faith is able to arm himself when he confronts all the devices of the devil. He will realize that the more effectively the power of God in Christ is asserted over the whole range of life, the more violently and desperately the evil will fight. 'Our fight is not against human foes, but against cosmic powers, against the authorities and potentates of this dark world, against the superhuman forces of evil in the heavens.'[1] But he is able to equip himself with the mighty weapon of the Spirit of God, made available to him through the atoning work of God in the Cross and Resurrection of Christ. 'Atonement', P. T. Forsyth insisted, 'is the answer to theodicy', and it answers it in the first instance in action, by enabling the man of faith to go forth to conquer evil, demonstrating more and more that its possibility of existence is only that of the impossible. If love is, in the familiar phrase, 'the impossible possibility', it makes clear as it succeeds in making itself manifest

[1] Ephesians vi. 12 (N.E.B.).

in this life, that the denial of love is the 'possible impossibility', which becomes the more impossible as the possibility of love is realized.

Living in the kind of world in which we have been set, there are many questions which we are able to raise whose answers are denied to us. We do not yet see all things in subjection to man, even the Messianic man of whom the Psalmist speaks.[1] But we do see Jesus, and we see Him, having suffered death, yet crowned with glory and honour, and we see Him as the one who stands for us all in that place. Seeing Him, and in seeing Him knowing His risen power, which means His conquest over the powers of sin, death and evil, we are able to know the answer to the fundamental question, 'How shall a man live?', and with patience and vigilance, we are able to persevere and, in persevering, able also to hope.

[1] Hebrews ii. 8, citing Psalm viii.

CHAPTER X

Agnosticism and Decision

It would not be surprising if the state of mind of many of those who have managed to follow this series of discussions thus far was something like this. They might allow that we have, at least, succeeded in proving one point, the point which was raised at the outset, that the whole question of the reality of God is not one which can be dismissed out of hand. It is a question which undoubtedly is raised by the nature of the human situation and one also which deserves much more thorough examination than men in these days are normally disposed to give to it. Yet the fact remains that it is a question about whose answer men are sharply divided from each other, more sharply divided in many ways than about any other question. If there is a case for belief in the Christian God, as we have tried to show, there is also a case against, and we are far from having demolished it. Does not this suggest that the absolutism which, in common with other convinced Christians, we have tried to inject into the discussion, is inappropriate? Are not all these things much more relative than we are prepared to allow? While men of good will remain sharply divided, is not the way of wisdom that of refusing to come down on one side or the other and trying to keep an open mind? Dogmatic and arrogant atheism may be without excuse, but does dogmatic and arrogant faith have much more to be said for it? Is not an attitude of agnosticism, which may well be combined with an attitude of grateful respect toward the Christian tradition, the only sensible one for fair-minded people to adopt? C. P. Snow, in a broadcast discussion, once described himself as a 'pious unbeliever'. What real objection can the Christian bring against this position?

This is, perhaps, the most common of all attitudes which, whether they openly admit it or not, people in Western lands have towards belief in God. It is notorious that, if what people say when challenged is to be taken with any seriousness, the number of self-confessed, strong-minded atheists, in Britain and the U.S.A. at least, appears to be very small. According to a survey conducted some years ago by the *Catholic Digest* in the U.S.A., 99 per cent of the people consulted said that they believed in God. The percentage would probably not be so impressive in Britain but Mass-Observation and similar surveys show figures not strikingly different. Yet while it is a good rule for intellectuals, and especially intellectual clergy, to put the most positive rather than the most negative, interpretation upon the religious deliverances of non-church-going people, it is permissible to inquire how far the God in whom many of these people claim to believe would be recognizable as the God of the Bible. He is someone vague, remote and uniformly and innocuously beneficent, One who tolerates with complacency differences of opinion about His reality because He does not affect life as it is lived in any significant way. Any man is entitled to his views about Him, but, on this matter more than any other, his views are his private affair, and the reasonable presumption is that one man's views on this subject are as good as those of the next. He is in no sense a 'jealous God', who will have mercy upon whom He will have mercy, and who takes the initiative in addressing man, whether man likes it or not. He is, rather, an 'optional' God, available for those who feel the need of Him or who are attracted to the idea as a speculation. This attitude has affected the outlook even of a large number of those who belong to the churches, who have made over their idea of God into their own amiable, tolerant and confused image and implied by their attitude, even when they have not explicitly stated it, that only those who find the idea helpful need concern themselves with it. The real basis of their community with their fellows is not belief or otherwise in this God but acceptability on other levels. This is, for all practical purposes, an attitude of agnosticism in relation to the Christian God but acceptance of relative, this-worldly, man-centred deities for certain limited purposes.

This easy-going and apparently sensible attitude is reinforced by three considerations of greater seriousness. The first is one we have already looked at briefly in other contexts. We claim to speak for the God whom Jesus Christ declared and we give reasons why it is right to regard His claim as exclusive. But we have acknowledged that there are other gods, who are followed with a zeal and devotion which are at least comparable with those which the Christian God inspires. What assurance can we really have that the Christian God is the true God in the way Allah is not, or that He is true in the way the Buddhist interpretation of existence is not. We were at pains earlier to insist that it is very hard to enter into the world of thought of these other faiths and to know what their teaching means in terms of Western experience and that, therefore, we should avoid sweeping generalizations about their relation to Christianity. But does not this strengthen the contention of the agnostic? If it is so hard to reach the position where one can make up one's mind about these things, does not that suggest that it is not very important that one should do so? Is not the sensible procedure, therefore, to have an attitude towards these conflicting religions rather like that of some enlightened British colonial administrators, who treat them all with official respect and private detachment and even with a touch of amusement about their pretensions, except, of course, when Christian missionaries, like Muslim nationalists, witch-doctors or Communists, start making public nuisances of themselves about their religion. It may be in bad taste to say so, but was Pilate so utterly unreasonable when, on a certain famous occasion, he asked what truth was without expecting an answer?

The second consideration is one which does not lend itself to much academic treatment but which carries a great deal of weight on the level of everyday observation. It is that a very large number of people appear to get on perfectly well without making up their minds about belief in God. Even in nominally Christian countries, a substantial proportion of the population, in many places probably a majority, seem to go through their lives either entirely indifferent to the religious issue or only raising it perfunctorily on occasion, generally when prompted to do so by social convention. Yet many of them are decent and likeable enough. They may have their faults, but who is without faults? Indeed, they are often pleasanter to be with than many diligent church workers. Consider a typical city dweller in a neighbourhood where the church has been practically non-existent for long generations, as in certain parts of London or Paris, for example. Not only does he seem to live tolerably satisfactorily without so much as raising the question of God but when he is addressed in Christian terms his reaction is no more than to look puzzled and embarrassed.

This attitude of bewildered indifference is paralleled, on a more self-conscious level, by that of more highly educated people. They are unable to become worked up about the whole issue of belief in God and the earnestness with which believers try to press the issue upon them appears either tiresome or slightly comic. They conclude that whether one is concerned with religious matters or obsessed with 'cosmic anxiety' depends largely upon temperament or upbringing. It is not something which is inescapably bound up with the human situation as such, a question which a man must answer if he is to discover his true nature and know how to live. This, in its turn, must mean that the God who is the object of this religious attention is someone a good deal less than the pious make him out to be. He cannot be the maker and ruler of all things, the One with whom in the last resort all men have to deal. This God is but one of the possible interpretations of the mystery of life which men devise. The Christian drama of salvation is a high-flown attempt to account for the various aspects of the moral life and to absolutize what is essentially relative. It is not the 'sacred history', the set of events which is decisive for our understanding of all the rest. It is only one curious and puzzling set of phenomena among others in the many-sided human story. The only possible attitude which the man of integrity will adopt to the Christian God and all His works is a wary agnosticism. It can be wistful or cynical, again according to temperament or according as to whether an individual has had pleasant or unpleasant experiences of the Christian community, but it will remain firmly non-committal.

A third consideration is that presented by our acute awareness in these days of the immensity of the universe in which we are set and the apparently ludicrous insignificance of our life on this little planet. This awareness, although not to the same degree, was present to the men of the Bible and produced very different conclusions, 'When I consider the heavens, the work of thy hands, what is man that thou art mindful of him and the son of man that thou visitest him?' But if a man does not recognize the heavens as the works of God's hands, it is very easy for him to conclude that belief in the Christian God is a form of human self-importance, and that, for all the protests of Christians to the contrary, faith is the most radical manifestation of anthropocentricism. The universe in which we are set is indeed mysterious, so mysterious that we cannot fathom its meaning. Why not admit it and cease to become so passionate and also so intellectually precise about matters where it is mere affectation to pretend that any real knowledge is given to men?

These difficulties, or very similar ones, must be present in the minds of many people today, whether they call themselves Christians or not. The characteristic modern temper is not so much positivistic as relativistic. Men are not really more convinced by the orthodoxies of 'scientism' than they are by those of theology. They are simply uncertain that there are any reliable landmarks. As we shall see, this attitude has its virtues as well as its defects and provides much valid criticism of various religious positions. Yet its difficulty, as always, is that it has not made a genuine effort to take the measure of the reality with which the believer claims to have been presented in faith.

[1] Psalm viii, 3-4.

Agnosticism and Decision

The distinctive characteristic of this reality is that it compels decision. Whether we like it or not, when we meet it, an adequate response to it is impossible without making up our minds about it, and making them up in such a way that our hearts and our wills are inevitably involved also. Indeed, its nature is such that it forces the issue upon us even when we would prefer to remain in a state of indecision. There are people who have a 'will to believe' and they are to be found in large numbers in the religious realm, but faith makes them see that this 'will to belief' is itself one of the great barriers which must be overcome if they are to attain to mature faith, because it can too easily lead them into the kind of belief which appears to 'satisfy their religious needs' while involving them in no act of commitment to a reality other than themselves which judges them. But a 'will not to believe' and a 'will not to make up one's mind' are at least equally prevalent, especially in our own time, and they provide no less of an impediment to true understanding. These are certainly much more of a barrier to faith than overt atheism, as theologians have frequently recognized, since overt atheism implies an element of self-commitment which is, at least, analogous to the commitment of faith.

From Biblical times onward, a temporizing indecision has been as much a barrier to faith as religious complacency. Men have always preferred not to make up their minds about God rather than directly to deny Him and have always resented His servants who tried to force them into situations where they had to make up their minds. This was the message of the prophets: 'How long halt ye between two opinions? If Yahweh be God, follow Him, but if Baal, then follow him.' It is, above all, the message of Jesus. When He comes, it is the *kairos*, the fulfilment of the times, and this cannot come without forcing decision upon men. Decision is the ceaseless theme of His teaching. 'He that is not for me is against me.' 'A house divided against itself cannot stand.' It is he who is prepared to launch out into the deep, to sell all his treasure for the pearl of great price, to make the venture of faith, who finds the kingdom. The great offence of the Cross consisted in the fact that it left men with no alternative but to say 'Yes' or 'No' to the God of Israel. From the point of view of faith it is seen as part of the illusion of unbelief that men are able to put this decision off 'until a more convenient season'. If this is 'the judgment of this present age', if the 'Prince of this present age' is now being cast out, we cannot remain in an attitude of cool detachment while the operation proceeds. We ourselves are part of the battle-ground where this struggle is taking place and we cannot dissociate ourselves from it. To try to do so means that we are, in fact, taking one side or the other.

It is a common enough human experience to be unable to reach full assurance of faith. Indeed, this is true of all men in greater or less degree. 'Lord, I believe, help thou mine unbelief' is the prayer which finds the clearest echo in the heart of most believers. There are also, it is true, various kinds of agnosticism. What may look like agnosticism may sometimes turn out to be a reluctance to trust the gods of this world which is based on a deeper faith in God than can yet find articulation, a faith in a 'God above God' analogous to the faith of Jesus Himself as He went into the darkness of the dereliction. We shall have more to say about this. But the kind of agnosticism which implies that no decision, and no corresponding commitment, in relation to the Christian revelation of God is necessary, has to prove that it has faced the Christian claim in its full magnitude, has done justice to it, and is yet able to show that it poses no fundamental issue for human life, so that it becomes possible to pass through life without having to define one's relation to it.

The reason why the man of faith finds this kind of agnosticism both understandable and unconvincing is that, at the very heart of the experience which has made him to be a believer is the awareness that the initiative in the encounter between him and God lies with God and not with himself. The Christian knowledge of God is always of God as the Lord, and that means knowledge of Him as One concerning whose existence agnosticism is no longer possible, because man has no independent standing-ground in relation to Him from which he can take up such a position. This, as we saw earlier, is what gave assurance of faith to Anselm when he was challenged by the unbeliever with the assertion that God was only an idea in his own mind. The lordship of God means His transcendence, which is not to be thought of in terms of 'remoteness' but of independent reality. God is the One who encounters us as the Other, whom we can neither call into being nor consign to non-being, who has His principle of existence within Himself. What is distinctive—from our human point of view, what is constitutive—of 'God' is precisely this independence of His which indicates that He is not the projection outside ourselves of our own sense of life's meaning or of the acuteness of our moral struggles. Linked with this are two other elements in the Christian knowledge of God, our consciousness of election and our conviction of sin and awareness of grace. 'You have not chosen me but I have chosen you' expresses our assurance about God in relation to men which is basic both to the Old Testament and the New. If the agnostic retorts that this can itself be no more than a subtle way in which the believer buttresses his sense of special destiny, the believer will agree that this is a possibility, as the history of the doctrine of election proves, but that the agnostic must at least recognize that, in intention, the doctrine is formulated in order to express the precise opposite. We know God as the One who chooses us, we do not know Him as one option among others which we as free and independent agents decide to accept. We would not have followed, we would not have dared to follow, if He had not already called.

The same reality governs our experience of sin and grace. It is hard to see how it is possible to avoid ethical agnosticism if one maintains a genuine theological agnosticism. It is true that the study of ethics has an important measure of autonomy in relation to the study of theology, but the more fundamental the ethical issue, the more difficult it becomes to avoid the theological issue. One cannot escape the suspicion that the triviality which appears frequently to beset the philosophical study of ethics in the universities of the Western world at a time when tremendous ethical issues confront men in that same world's wider life may be directly due to the theological agnosticism of many of its practitioners. It is true that many people have maintained that standards of conduct which were either formulated or received their sanction in the light of Christian belief have now justified themselves as, at least, sensible and desirable on empirical grounds and are now, therefore, more or less able to stand in their own right, independent of any supporting belief. Although they would have used different language, this was, more or less, the position of many Victorian agnostics who, in support of this contention, often strove to outdo churchmen in moral earnestness, sometimes with success. Much of the moral earnestness may have vanished, at least from formal discussion, but the claim remains. It is hard, however, to see what justification there is for it. Does public experience in the twentieth century go to support the contention not only that certain kinds of action are demonstrably better than others, which might be true, but that it is our duty to perform them, regardless of any unpleasant consequences to ourselves? If so, why do people so obstinately take the way either of cruel self-assertion or passive acquiescence in evil? It is hard to see how, on his own showing, the latter-day liberal agnostic can have any more than an aesthetic appreciation of the good, in Kierkegaard's sense, an appreciation which is powerless to resist the threats of militant evil and the self-destruction and ultimate chaos which it brings in its train. Christian faith is not only a belief that God reigns as transcendent Lord, who calls men according to His purpose. It is also a belief in God's holiness, which makes clear to us both the ultimate authority of the good and the extent to which we fall away from it. The fact that it makes clear to us the depth and range of our sin, in this sense, is itself an indication both of its reality and of the fact that indecision in relation to it is an ultimately untenable position.

'All have sinned and fallen short of the glory of God.' Most of us would prefer to deny this, or else to give a less radical interpretation of deficiencies and shortcomings. There is no conceivable human interest in trying to take these deficiencies and shortcomings with the seriousness with which Christian faith demands that we should. We should note also that it exposes any merely melodramatic interpretation of sin as thoroughly as it does any attempt to minimize it. Nothing aroused the indignation of Jesus more than the scrupulosity and the misplaced ethical meticulousness of the Pharisees. Jesus treated the consequence of sin as so grave that He obediently went to the crucifixion in order to make clear that its wages are indeed no less than death. Yet, in so doing, He made no less clear that the power which lies behind sin is futile, unreal and pathetic. The love which He revealed is shown to be the decisive power in the universe. This is what makes it impossible for men to stand aside from what He has done, as though it did not concern them. This is why it is not wrong for Christians to speak of God's grace in Christ as irresistible. It is irresistible, not in the sense that men are not still free to do a great deal to prevent its having its full way with them, but in the sense that it is a reality which has come into the world and whose influence is spreading through the whole of life and with which one day they will have to settle their account.

Perhaps we may go so far as respectfully to wonder whether the experience of many of our contemporaries who call themselves agnostic liberals does not go a fair distance to confirm the truth of this. There are many 'people of goodwill', to use that curious, ambiguous phrase, who are unable to confess to belief in God or who admit to being uncertain about the whole matter but who do so only with the tops of their minds, while in the depths of their being they are really committed to the same things to which believers are. This often becomes visible in a crisis when, unable as they are to say what they believe in, they are prepared to count their lives well lost for those things which are 'true and honourable and of good report'. They may wish to give a different interpretation of their actions, although part of our point is that in fact they are generally unable to, but from a Christian point of view it must look as though the potency of the reality represented by their baptism is far greater than they can themselves see, because their lives only make sense on the basis of the Christian reality. They are like those of whom Jesus spoke, who said 'I go not', and went, just as many of us who are faithful in church attendance but whose lives constantly deny our profession are those who say 'I go' and went not. This is why, when such people, as they not infrequently do, come to the point where they find themselves able to make open profession of faith, they do so not as though some new reality has descended upon them but with the recognition that they are at last able to see something which has been true for them all the time and by whose strength they have been secretly living.

We freely acknowledge that the agnostic liberal of the kind we have described will not accept this attempt to explain his situation and that, in conversation with him, the truth or otherwise of Christian faith has to be the subject of patient, critical discussion according to canons of truth which, whether consistently or otherwise, both parties are able to accept. Yet the understanding of the nature of the decision it compels which is given with Christian revelation itself is such that this is an interpretation which will look genuinely convincing from a Christian point of view. The nature of Christian revelation is such that it forces decision upon men. Those who bring forth the fruit of faith are likely to have made the decision of faith, even though they may have done so on a level of consciousness of which they are not fully aware. We say this with such confidence not because of any necessity of our natures as decision-making beings but because of the nature of the living God who enters the human situation and addresses us. It is He who, as soon as we recognize Him, exposes the unreality of our agnosticism.

II

The considerations brought forward by our agnostic at the beginning of this chapter remain before us, however. What is to be said of them in the light of what we have claimed for Christian decision? The question of the variety of the world's religions and their diverging claims has already been looked at and the need for caution in dealing with the whole matter has been sufficiently emphasized. It has to be observed that those who call attention to the existence of other religions and the problems they raise for faith often appear to be interested in doing no more than simply to call attention. They rarely seem able to go on to explain with more precision how these problems arise directly from the encounter of rival faith. Once again, we freely allow that there are many important issues as between the various faiths of the world which need further clarification, but, if one thing is certain, it is that they are likely to be resolved by those who have a basic commitment to one or other of them rather than by those who genuinely maintain right through an attitude of detached agnosticism. Further, the testimony of most students of the various religions of the world is that they differ from each other a great deal and force the student to make up his mind where he stands in relation to them. This is true just as much of apparently inclusive and accommodating Hinduism in its own peculiar way as it is of any other religion. Whether some forms of Confucianism may have points of affinity with Western agnosticism is arguable, and certainly no religion except to some extent the related religions of Judaism and Islam force the need for decision upon men in the Christian way, but ultimately what confrontation with the world's religions does for men is to sharpen the issues concerning the meaning of life and to impel them to seek their resolution rather than to encourage them to continue in a situation where their judgment remains suspended.

The question of the situation of those who, either through indifference or through inability to reach a decision, do not make open profession of belief in the Christian God, and who yet seem able to pass through life tolerably well deserves more discussion. This is partly because several different types of people are involved and partly also because many of these people are our contemporaries and our neighbours and it is particularly important that what we say should seem to be fair not only to ourselves but also to them.

For example, Christians are apt to say that these people, or at least many of them, are living on the spiritual capital built up in previous generations. They are not required to face the full implications of their present indecision or unbelief because they still enjoy some of the fruit of the faith of their fathers. Many of those misleadingly called 'the good pagans'[1] of our own day are, in a phrase used by John Baillie in his book *Invitation to Pilgrimage*, 'men of the afterglow'. Their lives still reflect the radiance of the Sun of righteousness, even though they may believe that, as far as they are concerned, that Sun has set. There may be truth in this from a Christian point of view, even though, as we shall see, what truth there is requires a good deal of qualification, but it has to be admitted that it is understandable that those who are in this position find it irritating to have it explained to them that they are only 'men of the afterglow', especially if the explanation is given with a touch of that pitying complacency which is not always absent from Christian comments of this kind. Many of our contemporaries may or may not be 'men of the afterglow' from a Christian point of view, but Christians cannot expect them to regard that as an adequate account of their situation. Nor, for that matter, should Christians regard it as adequate from their own point of view. The attachment many of them have to the good which we also cherish as Christians is much more positive and enduring than that fleeting image of the 'afterglow' suggests, with its implication that their attitude is one which finds the good only aesthetically pleasing. We need to take them more seriously than that and meet them with arguments and counter-questions rather than with unflattering explanations of how they contrive to be rather better than, on our theory, they have any right to be. As we have said before, it is a sure sign that there is something defective, from a Christian point of view, in any doctrine or theory whose protagonists find themselves compelled to disparage what is good in their neighbour in order to justify it. The Christian way is surely to cherish and rejoice in the good, and to give thanks to God for it, wherever it may be found.

We need to bear this particularly in mind when we recollect

---

[1] Misleading because they are not strictly pagans. The pagans worshipped gods of their own and were neither irreligious people nor sensualists.

how much Christians and their non-Christian contemporaries are members one of another in modern society. We share a common culture and a common way of life. Despite our differences in belief, we are very much like each other in innumerable ways. Besides, as we have reminded ourselves more than once, the unbelief of those outside finds an echo in the experience of those who are within the Christian community and any genuine faith on the part of Christians finds a response in those who do not make a Christian profession. A well-known writer who enjoyed working in a book-filled library was asked if he had read them all and replied that he had not but it did not matter. Books, he explained, were radio-active and they influenced him by their very presence. There is a measure of truth in this in relation to the life of faith. It is certainly true that one reason why so many people today are indifferent or confused is that those who purport to have the gift of faith have themselves become indifferent or confused in trying to make clear what it means in their lives. Their indirect influence has become unconvincing and ineffective.

Yet when all these qualifications have been made, we are still entitled to go on to put these considerations before those who claim that the indifference and unbelief of many reasonably well-disposed persons present a challenge to the faith of believers by demonstrating that faith is unnecessary. First, few of those who are indifferent show much evidence of having tried the Christian faith and found it wanting. Most of them have never troubled to give it any serious consideration at all. We have seen this to be true on the intellectual level in the failure of many opponents of Christian faith to give an account of how that faith came into being which is likely to convey to believers any conviction that these opponents have taken faith's measure. It is no less true on the level of ordinary, everyday experience. As a general rule, it can be said that many people who are indifferent to the religious dimension are superficial people in most other ways also. And without disparaging their virtues, it has to be noted that a good deal of their apparent success in life is often due to their irresponsibility. They have lightened the burden they carry through life and they have made a tacit agreement with themselves and with each other not to penetrate beyond certain levels of experience. They do not love or hate too much and do not concern themselves unduly with any matters which do not obviously obtrude themselves upon their consciousness. They are defective in imagination. They also undertake few commitments which are not well within their capacity and they distrust all ideas which disturb their settled ways. Sometimes this may involve a tolerant respect for religious practices, sometimes a genial contempt for them—depending on the conventions which prevail in their social group—but the basic attitude is the same in each case. The busy social life of many communities proceeds in this way, and many clubs and societies and, it has to be acknowledged, not a few churches, exist as semi-conscious conspiracies on the part of their members to keep everything superficial, to close the ranks against anyone who raises a fundamental issue and to maintain each other in mutual esteem. We may gratefully agree that such people can be pleasant enough in their own little world and can show many admirable qualities on secondary levels, whether they be 'middle-class' or 'working-class' qualities. But where do they present a challenge to faith, or, for that matter, to anything else? How can it be claimed that this half-life makes unnecessary our calling to be children of God? What answer do these people have to the charge that they simply avert their eyes from the dimension of mystery, in which both the inescapable tragedy and promise of life are to be found? In so far as people of this kind—and we are all, most of the time, people of this kind—show, in a crisis, qualities of faith, commitment and self-sacrifice, we can be grateful that they do so but still have to say that their previous way of life is neither justified nor explained by their display of such qualities. On the contrary, its inadequacy is exposed by them in the same way as it is by the sacrifice of Christ.

It may be argued that while this may be true of the great mass of superficially indifferent people, it is not necessarily true of reflective people who have genuine 'intellectual difficulties' and find themselves driven into a position of liberally-minded agnosticism. It must be admitted that there are kinds of agnosticism of which this is not true. It has been one of our own points that a reverent agnosticism, one which walks humbly in the presence of mystery and does not rush in with too ready answers, is the attitude to which revelation can most readily speak. And it has to be acknowledged that there are many people who, through tribulation or through their deep awareness of particular difficulties, cannot seem to reach faith. At the same time, we cannot blind ourselves to the fact that even much so-called reflective liberal agnosticism, perhaps indeed especially such agnosticism, shows an inconclusiveness of temper which, in itself, is the reverse of a challenge to faith. It is not an accident that the most characteristic academic vice is a temporizing indecision, which prefers to put off any judgment, from an examination to the Day of the Lord, till 'a more convenient season'. Those who have been given faith know enough about such agnosticism in their own souls to see this as a temptation to flee from reality rather than an awareness of reality which is of such depth as to prevent them from cherishing the alleged illusion of faith.

Secondly, what is it in the Christian interpretation of reality which the more enlightened and critically-minded agnostics have proved to be wrong and where is the more reliable and all-embracing view of reality from which they demonstrate it to be wrong? It must be acknowledged that faith is a gift, which it is not within our own powers either to evoke in ourselves or to bestow upon others, but, as we have tried to show, it is a gift which is able to provide its own validation. It leads us to decisive reality, which in its turn, is able to illuminate the rest of reality. It cannot be shown to be self-deception by any of the normal tests which are used to detect self-deception. What elements in the human situation have believers overlooked which are visible to those who do not believe and which should compel believers to resist the constraint of belief? Have they found a god, even though he may be frankly made in their own image, who is stronger than the God who was in Christ and who provides them with an adequate account of Christ which enables them to shrug off his demand that they reach a decision? 'Is there a God beside me? Yea there is no God: I know not any' says the second Isaiah (Isaiah xliv. 8). If the agnostic protests that this is the point, that there is no other God whom he has to offer, but the fact that that is so is no reason why he should accept the God of Israel, we may agree but still have to say that he has to demonstrate both why the God of Israel is unacceptable and how he finds it possible to live in his own apparent spiritual vacuum. If he is improperly described simply as a 'man of the afterglow', what is it from which he derives his conviction of life's meaning? Or if he argues that he does not know or that the question concerning meaning on any other than secondary levels eludes him, can he say, in the light of the experience of mankind in general and of men in modern Europe in particular, that it is possible to keep our spirits swept and garnished and yet to prevent seven legions of devils from entering and taking possession of them? If educated liberal agnostics find it possible to do so for themselves, is it, after all, because they are drawing on the vitality of the faith either of their fathers or of their neighbours?

Does the experience of modern Europe give any encouragement to the notion that whole societies are able to live for long on the basis of enlightened liberal agnosticism without being ridden by demons? This is not simply an argument for 'religion' as 'a social security'. It is to raise the question whether the human situation is such that the ultimate religious issue can be conveniently evaded by more than a small minority of people. What may be possible in King's College may not be so easy in society at large and, as is well known, even King's College has its chapel and exists in Christian Cambridge.

Thirdly, we have to ask even the most serious-minded agnostic what it is that he is refusing to make up his mind about, or what it is that he has rejected. As we saw in our second chapter, it is easy either to accept or to reject what we believe to be the Christian faith when what we are doing is nothing of the kind. It often appears then that our doubt is a form of liberation to us. It probably is, but it is liberation from false faith. It can become the proper agnosticism to which true faith speaks, but only if it enables us to give heed to what God in Jesus Christ really says. Too often, the agnostic uses this experience of genuine but limited liberation as an excuse for evading decision. For example, towards the close of one of the few modern books critical of Christian faith which shows theological knowledge, the author says this, 'Certainly, the Christian who loses his belief, and with it his imaginative vision of the world, has a colossal reorientation to carry out. He may feel like a child who has awakened not in the familiar friendly nursery in which he fell asleep, his parents within easy call, but in a desolate wilderness where no one knows of him, no one answers his cry.'[1] What is interesting about this statement is that Christian faith is assumed to be one of the cosy familiarities of childhood, in which one 'falls asleep'. It is also assumed, with a fine disregard of the real 'imaginative vision' of Christians who pay attention to the Bible, that the followers of Moses and Elijah and Amos and the tempted Jesus do not know 'the desolate wilderness'. Many forms of religion, including those which wear a Christian dress, do promote a feeling of childish security from which we need to be awakened to reality, but is it honest to justify agnosticism in relation to the *certitudo* of faith when all that has happened is that one has seen through this *securitas*? If a man really goes into the desolate wilderness of which Mr. Hepburn speaks, one thing is certain, that he will meet Jesus Christ there, as He wrestles with the mystery of evil and what He believes to be God's purpose. One of the things which make conversation between believers and liberal agnostics who claim to have 'seen through' the Christian faith peculiarly difficult, is that neither can take the other's good faith completely for granted. We have seen why this should be so in our discussion of the relation between faith and reason. A certain ironical quality must be inevitably present in such conversations.

It is because of this that the question concerning agnosticism and decision is, ultimately, best answered by each man in terms

[1] R. W. Hepburn, *Christianity and Paradox* (Watts, London), p. 152.

of his own experience. It is only true on some levels that the experience of each individual is unique. Each one of us is also a microcosm of the universe and this is especially true in our dealings with God, who is the king of all men and who has revealed Himself to mankind in Jesus Christ. The way in which God presents Himself to believers, if, as we believe, He really is God, is also the way in which, with due allowances for differences of circumstances and temperament and background, He is likely to reveal Himself to others also. At least, nothing fundamentally different is likely to enter into the relationship. If we show a proper understanding of the relationship, which means that we do not treat God as our private possession but recognizes that He prompts us into a relationship of sympathy and identification with our neighbour, we shall realize that our own dealings with God are likely to give us a reliable clue to the nature of His dealings with other men also.

It is this alone which enables believers to understand and to see the limitations of overt unbelief and also to see agnosticism, in so far as it is self-consistent, as a form of unbelief which is open to the same objections as all other forms of unbelief. Believers know how it is possible to deny God, ridiculous though it may be, because they themselves, even when they take His name upon their lips, constantly do so, in deed and in the intent of their hearts if not always in word. They also know how easy it is to drift into a position of practical agnosticism because they constantly find themselves doing this. What this generally means in their case is that they refuse to face the doubts and difficulties which time and time again confront man in a sinful world either because they are frightened that they might prove unanswerable or, at least equally, because they are frightened that they might be overcome and they be left with no justification for avoiding the painful and costly road of Christian duty. The fact that they can readily take refuge behind continuing formal professions of Christian belief, especially if they are parsons, does not make their agnosticism any the less real. It is of the same kind as that of the open agnostic. They find a place for faith, but not as the central reality. Any

Agnosticism and Decision

truth which it has must be caught up into a wider truth derived from other sources and it must not be taken seriously at its own evaluation of itself. It does not involve any radical commitment on their part, which involves their losing themselves that they might truly find themselves for the first time.

What the radical insight of faith makes us see is the opposite of what the agnostic imagines. He inevitably assumes that the believer has a pre-disposition to believe and is unable, out of fear for his own security, seriously to contemplate the possibility of unbelief. What the believer who has truly known the crucified and risen Christ sees, however, is that the characteristic, the conventional, human attitude, at least on the part of so-called 'mature' modern men, is that of agnosticism. Most men prefer not to have to make up their minds and to commit themselves. They prefer to take shelter behind established attitudes and institutions and to define life's meaning in their terms without having to take the risk of faith. As we have frequently seen, the chief way in which the devil works is not by giving men the power openly to deny God, it is by providing them with excuses which help them avoid having to make up their minds about the whole matter. Faith is the great miracle of human experience. In our unbelief we take this to mean simply that it is something which men find it particularly hard to accept, something which is accepted in a crude, external and irrational way and which cannot withstand honest scrutiny. But those who have known the miracle of faith see that it means very nearly the opposite of that. To call faith a miracle means that it comes from outside us when we do not expect it and would prefer to avoid it, that it is not generated by our own desire and that it comes as an illumination and as a grace. We know that it could not do for us what it has done if we honestly thought for a moment that it was no more than a very subtle psychological trick which we were playing upon ourselves. Its essence is that it is a gift, which comes from outside and provides us with what, of ourselves, we could not find. And it is the testimony of those who try to live the Christian life that the way in which faith vindicates its reality is by ceaselessly exposing the pretensions both of their piety and their agnosticism and by driving home to them, again and again, that it is only on God's terms, and never on their own, that it can continue to perform its transforming, healing work.

III

It is this insight which must, at every point, control the way in which, in these days, believers should try to speak of their faith to those who do not appear to share it. Christian apologists speak very frequently of the Church's failure in communication and think earnestly of ways in which they may become more effective in conveying their message to their fellows. This zeal is entirely right. No one can genuinely hear the Christian gospel without being made aware of his identification with his neighbour and without wanting to share all his good things, but supremely this greatest of gifts, with him. And certainly, as we have seen at many points throughout this discussion, those who lack faith show plenty of evidence of failure to understand what it is that the Bible and the men of faith are really saying. There has undoubtedly been a remarkable breakdown in communication between the Christian church and those outside it, despite all the painstaking efforts which have been made and despite all the apparent advantages to be derived from modern techniques of communication. Yet here more than anywhere else the truth holds that the most effective way in which communication to others becomes possible is that those who wish to communicate should ensure that, in the deep places of their own being, they should themselves believe in what they wish to transmit. Nowhere does the mysterious 'bush-telegraph' which exists in the realm of ideas operate more effectively than in the matter of faith and, in the modern world, where we all have such sensitive antennae reaching out towards our neighbours, this is particularly true. One of the chief reasons why, at least by their own standards, the churches have counted for comparatively little in the Western world over the last few generations is that, in all kinds of subtle and indirect ways, they have served notice to all who have eyes to see that they have not been altogether sure of the Christian faith themselves. True faith is inescapable, but it cannot be effectively simulated. To try to speak in a confident tone of voice and to keep all one's self-questionings in the background will not serve to convince men. Catholicism has long mastered that art, and in our own time conservative Evangelicalism has diligently practised it and, although it may succeed in impressing some, it cannot make much headway against the whole mood of a generation. Faith must be genuine, but where it is it inevitably spreads and a little is enough to leaven the lump of a whole society. No one who comes in contact with it can be immune from its quickening influence. This is why, although Karl Barth might have done much more than he has done to help clear unnecessary mis-understandings out of the way of faith, the very fact that the reality of living faith in the lordship of God in Christ springs out of the pages of his writings in the same way as it does through personal encounter with him, means that the Gospel has been more effectively communicated to the men of our own time through his work than it has through all our anxious efforts at 'demythologization', dramatization and populariza-tion. Ultimately, what men really want to hear from their fellows, men of like nature with themselves as they are, is whether they have found genuine assurance concerning God's reality. If they discover that their fellows have, then they know that, whether they like it or not, they also will have to take seriously the possibility that God may become a reality in their own lives.

The truth of this is confirmed by the fact that living faith cannot exist without the expression of humility and love and without pointing men, not to itself, but to the Christ who is its source. The connection between faith and humility cannot be too emphatically stressed, especially as its application to the form which our evangelistic efforts should take is not always clearly seen. To try over-anxiously to convince our neighbour of the truth of the Christian faith, at almost any price and by using

any instrument which lies to hand to do so, is a form of dangerous pride which obscures the nature of the God we proclaim
and the proper human relationship to Him. It implies that God
is the kind of being who can be 'sold' to men by psychological
intimidation and that He depends for His ability to convince on
human powers of salesmanship. This attitude, especially in these
days when the tempation to use the sinister methods of mass-
suggestion and 'saturation-propaganda' lie readily to hand,
comes very close to the efforts to compel belief by force which
we are all accustomed to deplore in the inquisitorial practices
of men in previous ages. God has placed us in a world of
mystery, where the answers to life's deepest questions are not
obvious. They are only given in faith and only to those who
take trouble to turn aside to see. We can see that one reason for this
mode of the divine revelation is that it prevents men from
taking God's name upon their lips too lightly, so that they
conceal from themselves and their neighbours that 'it is a
terrible thing to fall into the hands of the living God'. This is an
insight which is essential if they are to know how costly and
how blessed the divine grace is.

There can be no doubt that one of the chief unnecessary
obstacles which have been placed in the way of belief for men
today is that of the misplaced confidence of the spokesmen of
the Christian community in claiming the authority of revelation
for what are no more than human opinions. We saw earlier
that the dogmas of the Christian faith must on no account be
presented in what is commonly called a dogmatic way. It is no
less important to see that the essential dogmas are very few in
number. Indeed, they probably boil down to no more than an
affirmation of what the men of the Bible meant when they
spoke of the lordship of Jesus Christ. One of the salutary services
of modern relativism to theology, which theology should have
been strong enough to accept more readily and more constructively than it normally has, has been to make clear to men
that the area of uncertainty which surrounds the basic affirmations of faith is much larger than most Christians had been
disposed to believe in previous ages. This does not mean that

high degrees of authority cannot be properly claimed for many kinds of Christian statement which are not the ultimate truth, but the nature and limits of this authority need to be clearly understood. There can be little doubt, for example, that one proper consequence of our awareness of the greatly enlarged size of the physical universe and the infinitesimally small place occupied within it by man and his world has been to set the familiar doctrinal disputes between Christians in a different perspective. It may not be sufficient to reduce to insignificance the argument between those, for example, who believe that infants should be baptized and those who believe that only those of years of discretion should be baptized but it should, at least, prompt both sides to see that this may be a matter about which finality of judgment is not given to men and that in a world of mystery it is more important that those who believe that if we are buried with Christ we shall also rise with Him should maintain fellowship with each other than that they should go their separate ways. And what is true of this, division is also true, in their degree, of many other long-standing divisions, not least those between Protestants and Catholics.

Christians need in these days to be recalled sharply to their proper attitude of humility in relation both to each other and to their neighbours who do not appear to have the gift of faith. The Christian church has become by now a very ambiguous institution, whose light rarely shines before men with sufficient clarity to enable them to see the good works of those who belong to it and glorify their Father which is in heaven. And Christians have to accept the fact that God has placed men in a world of mystery, where some, through no merit of their own, can see His hand at work and know the blessing of faith, whereas others cannot. The task of believers is not to make the way of faith more difficult for those outside their company. They must be rigorously careful not to ask them to consent to more than that which is truly necessary for belief. They must make the most limited of claims, in terms of prestige or money or attention, for the Church as an institution, asking no favours of men because they have the gift of faith. True faith always makes us debtors to our neighbours. All the time, their concern must be to point away from themselves to Christ, and to be patient with their neighbours if they fail to see the glory of God in His face. Christians must always remember that if God continues to be patient with their neighbours, as He does with Christians themselves in their repeated sinfulness, they deny Him if they lose patience with their neighbours in zeal for His name. Once again, the record of the Christian community as the custodian of revelation is too ambiguous for any of its spokesmen to dare to take any other line. It could be that the continuing inability of the Church as an institution to commend itself readily to men in several countries, especially in Britain, is itself an act of God's merciful patience to His people. Are churches ready to receive great popularity without spiritual peril? The frighteningly easy popularity which many churches have achieved in the U.S.A. in our own time, without undergoing any obvious reformation and real spiritual renewal, indicates clearly enough the dangers of becoming an institution for the purveyance of 'cheap grace'.

This does not mean that Christians need know any frustration or show any improper reserve about witnessing to their faith. The primary, and ultimately the only decisive way, in which faith works is through love. And whether our neighbour comes to share our faith or not, we are free to express the love of Christ in our dealings with him. It is true that a reciprocity is possible in the relations of fellow-believers which is not always open to believers and non-believers in their dealings with each other—it is this which should make the reality of the Church such a means of grace—but this does not prevent us from expressing the love of Christ to all men. Where this love, the disinterested service of the true well-being of our neighbour in the light of Christ, is present, a new fact has entered the world, to which no one, whatever his professed belief, can remain indifferent. To the extent to which he is a living, responsible human being, he has to adjust himself to it, whether he likes it or not, as he has to the forgiveness, the peace and the joy which follow from it. Believers know that they have passed from death to life because the impossible possibility has been realized, they love each other (1 John iii. 14). In the presence of this love, the unbeliever has to recognize the presence of life conquering death and, do what he will, he has to abide in this love.

This is the answer to the question which men frequently ask today of Christians. 'How can I enter the circle of faith?' To reply, as cautious Christians are disposed to do, 'Only God can admit you to that circle' is true but it is not the only thing which can be usefully said. For God Himself has taken the initiative in helping men to enter the circle of faith. He has sent His son, Jesus Christ. This is why, when we speak of divine revelation, we point men to the figure of Jesus Christ, in the confident hope that, as God has shown us the light of the knowledge of His glory in the face of Jesus Christ, so He will be able to do the same for our neighbour. Yet, perhaps, we in the Christian community, and not least those of us who are called to be theologians and ministers of the Word, need to see that our ministry is not completely fulfilled when we have pointed away from ourselves to Christ. We can point men to Jesus and they may conclude, at best, that he was a religious genius—whatever they may choose to make of religion—of remarkable critical insight who worked out the inner logic of the human situation more consistently and heroically than anyone else. That He was the Christ, the Son of the living God, is something which flesh and blood cannot reveal to them. But those who have been given the insight to see that He is the Son of God are able to do more. They are able, by their identification with Christ as He identified Himself with man, to stand along-side their neighbour in love. Here, above all other places, we must be clear that this love is the fruit of faith, which, in its turn, is evoked only by God's revelation in Christ. It demonstrates its reality by its self-forgetfulness, its identification with Christ and His will. Nothing more effectively blocks revelation than that those who claim to speak in Christ's name should so mis-understand Him as to put their human attempt at love in His place. Yet this, in its turn, must not be allowed in these days to obscure the other side of the truth, that faith without love is like sounding brass and a tinkling cymbal. Too much of our preaching sounds like these for us to dare to forget it. Men are tired of the words of Christians about Christ and they no longer give heed to them. Yet the world has never hungered and thirsted more for the life-giving love of Christ. That love has been shed abroad in our hearts. We are free to share its abundance with all whom we can reach.

Index

223

Index

Ecclesiastes, 21, 156
Ecumenism, 75, 125, 191-2
Elijah, 81 n., 91
Eliot, George, 55
Encyclicals, Papal, 19
Enlightenment, The, 37, 54, 128, 146
Ephesians, letter to, 96, 124-5, 133, 176, 194
Evangelicalism, 40, 137, 217
Existentialism, 30, 47, 65, 92, 153, 155
Exodus, 90-1, 118

Farmer, H. H., 78, 134
Fascism, 153
Feuerbach, Ludwig, 36
Fitch, Robert M., 190 n.
Forster, E. M., 137, 138 n.
Forsyth, P. T., 70, 169, 175, 194
Foster, Michael, 17 n.
Frank, Erich, 51, 62, 63
Freud, Sigmund, 36 n., 129, 134, 147, 150
Fundamentalism, 19, 42

Gaunilo, 64
Genesis, 89
Germany, 182, 191
Gilkey, J. Langdon, 114 n.
Gnostics, 22, 119
Greece, the Greeks, 24, 46, 47, 48, 59, 62, 78, 97, 152, 156, 158-9

Halevy, Daniel, 181 n.
Hathorn, Richard, 148 n., 152
Hebrews. See Israelites
Hebrews, letter to, 96, 126, 179, 195
Heidegger, M., 153
Heim, Karl, 54 n., 55 n., 60 n.
Hendry, G. S., 17 n.
Hepburn, R. W., 213
Hinduism, 73, 79, 82-3, 207

Hodges, H. A., 39
Hosea, 15
Hoskyns, E. C., 86, 163
Hulme, T. E., 56
Humanism, 24, 101, 102, 116, 133, 140-1, 148
Hume, David, 52, 53
Huxley, Aldous, 56

India, 145
International Missionary Council, 75
Isaac, 89-90
Isaiah, 15, 93, 120, 212
Islam, 74, 77, 79, 80, 124, 145, 198, 207
Israel, the Israelites, 81-2, 88-95, 97, 101-2, 116, 118, 120, 121, 145, 159, 177-8

Jaeger, Werner, 28
Jeremiah, 194
Jews. See Israel or Judaism
Joad, C. E. M., 40
Joan of Arc, 180-1
Job, 91, 156, 170, 171-2, 178
John, Gospel of, 14, 96, 103-5, 107, 110, 111, 127, 133, 159, 162, 172, 179, 192, 221
Jonah, 91
Judaism, 44, 73, 91, 108 n., 139, 179-80, 207

Kant, Emmanuel, 47, 54-5, 60, 63
Kierkegaard, Sören, 43, 47, 49, 76, 121, 204
Kraemer, H. H., 75

Laski, Marghanita, 24 n.
Lewis, C. S., 62 n.
Lightfoot, R. H., 86, 114 n.
Linguistic Philosophy, 29-30, 47, 155
Lisbon Earthquake 170
Luke, Gospel of, 96, 158
Luther, Martin, 69, 176

224

Index

Index